BEFORE DINOSAURS

In late 1966, *One Million Years B.C.* opened in British cinemas and became a smash hit. The American release in 1967 followed suit, where Raquel Welch and Ray Harryhausen's dinosaurs were received with great aplomb. It was one of Hammer Film's greatest hits and broadened the studio's appeal, as before this the studio was predominantly known for their gothic horror output.

During shooting of *B.C.*, producer Michael Carreras was already thinking of a... let's say "spiritual sequel." The inspiration for a similar film wasn't because any type of great story needed to be told, or even because Carreras thought that *B.C.* would be a hit. Another film was whipped up simply because costs on *B.C.* needed to be offset, and so Hammer wanted to come up with a similar picture that could reuse the sets and costumes from *B.C.*

Carreras approached Martine Beswick, playing the Rock Tribe's Nupandi, during the shoot and asked her if she'd want to be the "queen" in the next film. She was delighted until she asked him the title and he replied, "Slave Women of the White Rhino."

Indeed, this was *Prehistoric Women's* original title. The resultant film one could consider a watered down hybrid of *B.C.* and *She*. While the titular characters are indeed cave women, they all speak English. There are no prehistoric creatures, save for the White Rhino, which is mostly immobile throughout the picture (it's more of a magical totem rather than a living creature).

RULED THE EARTH

In 1969, before *B.C.*'s sequel had even been released, Hammer put out a double-bill rerelease of *B.C.* and *She*.

The film starred Michael Latimer as David Marchant, a British safari guide in Africa. While hunting a wounded leopard in a forbidden part of the jungle, he stumbles across a tribe that worships a sacred White Rhino. Just as the tribe is about to execute Marchant in front of the life-like totem, he reaches out to grab its horn. Time stands still, lightning flashes, and a crack opens in the cave wall.

Marchant either finds himself in the prehistoric past or an alternate dimension (we don't know which) inhabited by the titular characters. Marchant quickly becomes imprisoned by a tribe of brunettes, ruled over by Queen Kari (Beswick's character). The brunettes rule over the blondes, and when Marchant refuses to be Kari's male concubine, Marchant is imprisoned with a blonde named Saria.

As you can imagine, Marchant and Saria fall in love, which naturally means that Saria is slated to be sacrificed to the White Rhino. Just as she is about to be sacrificed, the imprisoned cavemen and blondes break free to wage war on Kari and her followers. The White Rhino comes to life and rams Kari with its horn, killing her. A storm brews as Marchant says a sorrowful goodbye to Saria.

He awakens in front of the White Rhino statue in the present, and the tribe that was about to execute him watches in shock as the statue crumbles. The natives declare it was a false god that Marchant has freed them from. He is allowed to be let

go. Back at his camp, he finds a new visitor named Sara who looks just like Saria...

There's a lost cut of *Prehistoric Women* that runs 74 minutes called *Slave Girls* (the UK title). You see, the original plan was for *Prehistoric Women* (which ran 91 minutes) to be the 'A' feature on a double bill with a rerelease of *The Old Dark House* (1963). Hammer decided the film wasn't main feature material, edited it down to 74 minutes, and made it the support feature for *The Devil Rides Out* (1968) under the title of *Slave Girls*. The version known as *Prehistoric Women* was released in the U.S. uncut at its full length.

In hindsight Carreras, who also produced, wrote, and directed the film, commented several times that he had wished he'd added in the comic book bubbles from the *Batman* TV series to the fight scenes since it was, to him, a "comic book film."

Hammer produced a few more glamour pictures based off of *She* and *B.C's* success, including *The Viking Queen* (1967) and *Vengeance of She* (1968). Carreras recalled that these Hammer Glamour pictures were profitable for what they were, but didn't have the staying power of *B.C.* or their gothic horror output.

PRESSBOOK

FEATURES

EDITORIAL...2

BEFORE DINOSAURS RULED THE EARTH A look at *Prehistoric Women*...6

MINI PREHISTORIC WOMEN PRESSBOOK...9

WHEN DINOSAURS RULED THE EARTH Original casting choices for the cavepeople and prehistoric beasts alike, unfilmed and deleted scenes, and more....13

MINI WHEN DINOSAURS RULED THE EARTH PRESSBOOK...31

SEQUELS THE WORLD FORGOT *Creatures the World Forgot's* surprising link to David Allen's *The Primevals*...39

MINI CREATURES THE WORLD FORGOT PRESSBOOK...53

WHEN THE EARTH CRACKED OPEN Discover the last caveman movie that Hammer never made ...57

AFTER DINOSAURS RULED THE EARTH Explore films inspired by the success of Hammer's cavepeople pictures ...62

THE LOST FILMS FANZINE PRESENTS
MOVIE MILESTONES #2 OCTOBER 2020

EDITOR AND PUBLISHER: JOHN LEMAY/BICEP BOOKS
SPECIAL CONSULTANT: KYLE BYRD

MOVIE MILESTONES IS A SPECIAL MAGAZINE PUBLISHED IN CONJUNCTION WITH THE LOST FILMS FANZINE. THE COPYRIGHTS AND TRADEMARKS OF THE IMAGES FEATURED HEREIN ARE HELD BY THEIR RESPECTIVE OWNERS. MOVIE MILESTONES ACKNOWLEDGES THE RIGHTS OF THE CREATORS AND THE COPYRIGHT HOLDERS OF THE IMAGES THEREIN AND DOES NOT SEEK TO INFRINGE UPON THOSE RIGHTS. IMAGES AND MATERIALS USED HEREIN ARE PUBLICITY IMAGES THAT WERE MADE AVAILABLE FOR MAGAZINE USE AT THE TIME OF THE RESPECTIVE FILMS RELEASES AND ARE USED IN THE INTEREST OF EDUCATION AND PUBLICITY. ARTICLES AND TEXT WITHIN THE MAGAZINE ARE © THEIR RESPECTIVE AUTHORS AND MAY NOT BE REPRINTED WITHOUT PERMISSION. MOVIE MILESTONES IS NOT ASSOCIATED WITH HAMMER FILM PRODUCTIONS, TWENTIETH CENTURY FOX, WARNER BROS-SEVEN ARTS, COLUMBIA PICTURES, OR ANY OF THE PRODUCTION COMPANIES INVOLVED IN PRODUCING OR DISTRIBUTING THE FILMS ON HOME VIDEO. CONTACT THE EDITOR @ jplemay@plateautel.net

EDITORIAL

Hello and welcome to the second issue of *Movie Milestones*, a subsidiary of *The Lost Films Fanzine* that celebrates movie anniversaries with an emphasis on their more uncelebrated aspects. Before we go any further, I have a confession to make. What became this issue was originally supposed to be a part of the *One Million B.C.* tribute in Issue #1. It had been my hope to celebrate a joint anniversary for *B.C.* and *When Dinosaurs Ruled the Earth* (henceforth *WDRTE*), which, believe it or not, turns 50 in October of 2020! (I saw the film when it was only about 28 years old, so I find it hard to believe myself that's it been a full 22 years since I first saw it!)

You might ask why I didn't simply make one big monster issue out of both (as I did with the 100 page Fall issue of *The Lost Films Fanzine*) and the answer is economics. Boring, I know, but I'm sure some of you are curious so I'll tell you. 100 pages of premium color would mean a rather expensive fanzine. You see, there's a big difference between basic color, which is what *The Lost Films Fanzine* prints in, and premium color, which I felt *Movie Milestones* deserved at least one edition in. So, yes, for the sake of economics, what was originally one issue got split into two—also because there's a lot of unmade aspects to these films!

And though I love Hammer's *One Million Years B.C.*, I've always loved *WDRTE* more. Maybe it's because I saw *One Million Years B.C.* when I was about eight, but saw *WDRTE* at twelve, the perfect age to appreciate

its attributes. I wasn't grown up enough to lose interest in dinosaurs (but, then again, I'm still not) and I was old enough to truly appreciate Victoria Vetri and her beautiful co-stars. As much as I loved the film, I mourned the fact that there was an alternate cut. One in which Victoria Vetri's character, Sanna, got naked...

For many years, for me, that was a "lost film," or "lost cut" at least. The film was my new *Destroy All Monsters* (1968). You see, as a ten year old growing up in the 90s, *Destroy All Monsters* was THE lost Godzilla movie at the time. It was the Holy Grail for kids like me as it was the only Godzilla movie to not have a U.S. VHS release.

Well, in my late teens, the uncut *WDRTE* was my new movie-Holy Grail. I searched high and low for it until I finally found a DVD on EBay. The cut scenes were easy to spot, because whenever they came on, the DVD quality would diminish considerably. Only a few years later, Warner Bros would accidentally release the uncut version on DVD!

What had happened was that they had forgotten that the U.S. cut was censored, and they used the original master for the new DVD (which was still "Rated G", by the way).

Another reason I love *WDRTE* is that it offers a fun little inverse to *B.C.* where the female is the lead rather than the male. Yes, Raquel Welch was a major focus in *B.C.*, but we as the audience followed Tumak, Loana was a part of his journey. *WDRTE* is the opposite, as we follow Sanna. Not only that, several times Sanna rescues Tara instead of the other way around. Furthermore, Sanna is from the primitive Rock Tribe while Tara is from the more peaceable Sand Tribe (which might as well be the Shell Tribe).

The music has a more whimsical fantasy quality to it than *B.C.*'s score did as well. The landscapes are also softer in many ways. Yes, both *WDRTE* and *B.C.* were filmed in the same locations in the Canary Islands, but the studio sets and matte paintings have a stark contrast to the rocky landscape of the Canaries. There are lush jungles in *WDRTE*, while there were none in *B.C.* And while *B.C.* did have a few beach scenes, the Sand Tribe's beach seems much more welcoming.

Everything discussed in the previous paragraph was in stark contrast to director Val Guest's intent. He hated the matte paintings because he wanted the film to have a documentary feel to it. Instead, it turned into something more fantastical than even *B.C.* had been!

THE LOST FILMS FANZINE PRESENTS MOVIE MILESTONES #2

My love for *WDRTE* eventually led to my tracking down its "sequel," *Creatures the World Forgot*, shortly after acquiring the uncut version of *WDRTE*. Even though I knew that *CTWF* was sans any saurians (save for a python), as a completest I still had to see it.

At the time, the film was a bit more obscure than it is now. Though it was late to the digital video disc party, it finally got a DVD release in 2011. If memory serves I bought an OOP, ex-rental VHS copy of the film in 2009.

And, to my surprise, I enjoyed it. Perhaps it was because my expectations for the film were so low. Everything I had read about the film was mostly negative. But, if one can get past the lack of dinosaurs, *CTWF* isn't that bad.

In my humble opinion, it's one of those unloved films that has a worse reputation than it deserves, much like the perennial "red headed step child." Heck, even 1967's *Prehistoric Women* gets more love than *CTWF*!

A little late in the game, after I split issue #1 in two, I decided to show this forgotten film a little more love. So rather than this issue being solely a 50th anniversary tribute to *WDRTE*, I now think of it as a joint 50th anniversary tribute to *WDRTE* and *CTWF*... albeit a slightly early one where the latter is concerned.

CTWF was released in April of 1971, which makes this issue's debut just six months shy of celebrating its true anniversary. The film reportedly did alright its first week of release and then had a steep drop off. And yet, despite that, Hammer still had plans for more caveman films to follow (ones with dinosaurs, too, and some without).

In the spirit of *The Lost Films Fanzine*, I hope you enjoy this look not only at what the films are, but what they could have been, the unfilmed scenes we'll never see, and the sequels left unmade...

Men— beaten into submission... turned into slaves by a kingdom of

AVAILABLE AS
MAT 110
137 lines x 1 column
1 column x 9¾ inches

AVAILABLE AS
MAT 208
142 lines x 2 columns
(284 lines)
2 columns x 10½ inches

CAST

Kari.......... Martine Beswick	Ullo.......... Sydney Bromley
Saria.......... Edina Ronay	Arja.......... Frank Hayden
David......... Michael Latimer	Colonel Hammond.. Robert Raglan
Amyak........ Stephanie Randall	Mrs. Hammond...... Mary Hignett
Gido.............. Carol White	Head Boy........ Louis Mahoney
Luri...... Alexandra Stevenson	High Priest........ Bari Jonson
First Amazon..... Yvonne Horner	Jakara............ Danny Daniels
John............... Steven Berkoff	

PRODUCTION STAFF

Produced and
  Directed by..Michael Carreras
Screenplay by.... Henry Younger
Director of
  Photography..... Michael Reed
Music Composed
  By .... Carlo Martelli
Musical
  Supervisor.... Philip Martell
Choreography.... Denys Palmer
Art Director...... Robert Jones
Supervising Editor..James Needs
Costume Designer .... Carl Toms
Production
  Manager....... Ross Mackenzie
Editor .... Roy Hyde

Assistant
  Director...... David Tringham
Camera
  Operator...... Robert Thomson
Continuity ...... Eileen Head
Dubbing
  Editor...... Charles Crafford
Sound Mixers...... Sash Fisher,
                   A.M.I.E.E.
                   Len Shilton
Make-up Super-
  visor...... Wally Schneiderman
Hairdressing
  Supervisor...Olga Angelinetta
Wardrobe
  Mistress........ Jackie Breed

CinemaScope   Color by De Luxe
A Seven Arts-Hammer Production
Distributed by 20th Century-Fox Film Corp.
Running time: 91 minutes

POSTERS & ACCESSORIES

1-SHEET
40 x 60

WINDOW CARD

INSERT CARD

ALSO AVAILABLE
22 x 28
SET OF (8) 11 x 14's
SET OF B/W STILLS

COPYRIGHT MCMLXVI TWENTIETH CENTURY FOX FILM CORP., PRINTED IN U.S.A.

PUBLICITY

THREE NEWCOMERS STAR IN JUNGLE ADVENTURE, "PREHISTORIC WOMEN"

"Prehistoric Women," a jungle thriller in CinemaScope and De Luxe color, presents three young newcomers in the starring roles -- Martine Beswick, Edina Ronay and Michael Latimer. The picture, which opens on _____ at the _____ Theatre, is a Seven Arts-Hammer Production released by 20th Century-Fox and was produced and directed by Michael Carreras.

"Prehistoric Women" tells the story of a young English big game hunter who, tracking down a wounded leopard, enters a sacred area of jungle. There, mysteriously breaking an ancient legend, he frees a tribe not only from a spiritual bondage that had imprisoned them since prehistoric times, but also from their slavery to a prehistoric tribe of Amazon women.

Martine Beswick, a tall, shapely, dark-haired and dark-eyed Jamaican actress, plays the cruel Queen of the Amazons. It is her first starring role, though she is the only actress ever to appear in more than one James Bond film -- "From Russia with Love" and "Thunderball."

Petite, blonde Edina Ronay has appeared steadily on television and has also appeared in several films, including "Bunny Lake Is Missing," "The Big Job" and "A Study in Terror."

Michael Latimer is the lucky leading man who makes his film debut surrounded by more than fifty beautiful girls.

* * * * *

SCENE MATS

Martine Beswick, as Queen of the Amazons, relaxes in her luxurious, if primitive, boudoir in "Prehistoric Women," a Seven Arts-Hammer production in CinemaScope and De Luxe Color released by 20th Century-Fox, coming on _____ to the _____ Theatre.   MAT 2C

Martine Beswick and Michael Latimer in a scene from "Prehistoric Women," a Seven Arts-Hammer production released by 20th Century-Fox.   MAT 2A

GREATER THAN 'ONE MILLION YEARS B.C.'

WHEN DINOSAURS RULED THE EARTH

Director: Val Guest *Script*: Val Guest (based upon a story by J.G. Ballard) *SPFX Director*: Jim Danforth *Music*: Mario Nascimbene *Cast*: Victoria Vetri (Sanna) Robin Hawdon (Tara) Patrick Allen (Kingsor) Imogen Hassall (Ayak) *Release Date*: October 1, 1970 *Runtime*: 100 Minutes

Plot: Sanna, a blonde girl amongst the mostly dark haired Rock Tribe, is blamed for recent atmospheric phenomena. She escapes her tribe and is rescued by Tara, of the kindly Sand Tribe. Kingsor, a high priest of the Rock Tribe, pursues Sanna to the Sand Tribe and so she must flee. Tara goes out in search of her. The lovers are reunited, but are captured by Kingsor and his men. The atmospheric phenomena (the formation of the Moon) intensifies into a tidal wave that kills Kingsor and his followers. Tara, Sanna, and their friends are able to live on in peace.

THE LOST FILMS FANZINE PRESENTS MOVIE MILESTONES #2

WHEN DINOSAURS RULED THE EARTH

Above and page opposite: Several different release posters for *WDRTE*.

As with any movie, there are varying reports on how this film came to be. It is said that Warner Bros. approached Hammer about an un-official follow-up to *B.C.* and the project was in the planning stages by 1968.

However, evidence to the contrary points to Hammer starting the project, not Warners. Michael Carreras was at work on the sequel by May of 1967. To get the ball rolling, he had a poster drawn up to garner interest. Supposedly, all it took was the poster to sell Warner Bros-Seven Arts on the film! Keep in mind, there was no script yet. But, then again, did there really need to be if it was to be a simple follow-up to *B.C.*? After all, so long as there were stop-motion dinosaurs and cave girls that was all that mattered.

Aida Young, an associate producer on *B.C.*, was promoted to the main producer on the sequel. Step one was finding someone to begin the story, so she chose one of her favorite sci-fi authors: J.G. Ballard. She had been trying to get Hammer to adapt some of Ballard's sci-fi stories for years (notably his 1962 novel *The Drowned World* about global warming causing floods).

Ballard accepted the offer to write the *B.C.* sequel because he was curious about the British film industry. In his autobiography, *Miracles of Life*, he recollected that, "I turned up at the Wardour Street offices of Hammer, to be greeted in the foyer by a huge Tyrannosaurus rex about to deflower a blonde-haired actress in a leopard-skin bikini. The credits screamed 'Curse of the Dinosaurs!'" [page 226]

"Had the film already been made?" Ballard thought to himself looking at the poster. [Ibid] Ballard asked Young about it and she told him that they had already changed the title to *When Dinosaurs Ruled the Earth*.

Details of the meeting between Ballard, Young, and Tony Hinds are vague but tantalizing. For starters, it seems there was some talk of bringing back Raquel Welch (and therefore Loana) that failed. Furthermore, at the time, the lead actress being eyed was Czech and didn't speak English, which really didn't matter all things considered.

Young kicked off the talk by explaining to Hinds the storyline of Ballard's *Drowned World* (I still think this was a backdoor ploy on Young's part to interest Hinds in a *Drowned World* movie). Hinds' response to the story: "Water?

Above: J.G. Ballard's novel *The Drowned World*.

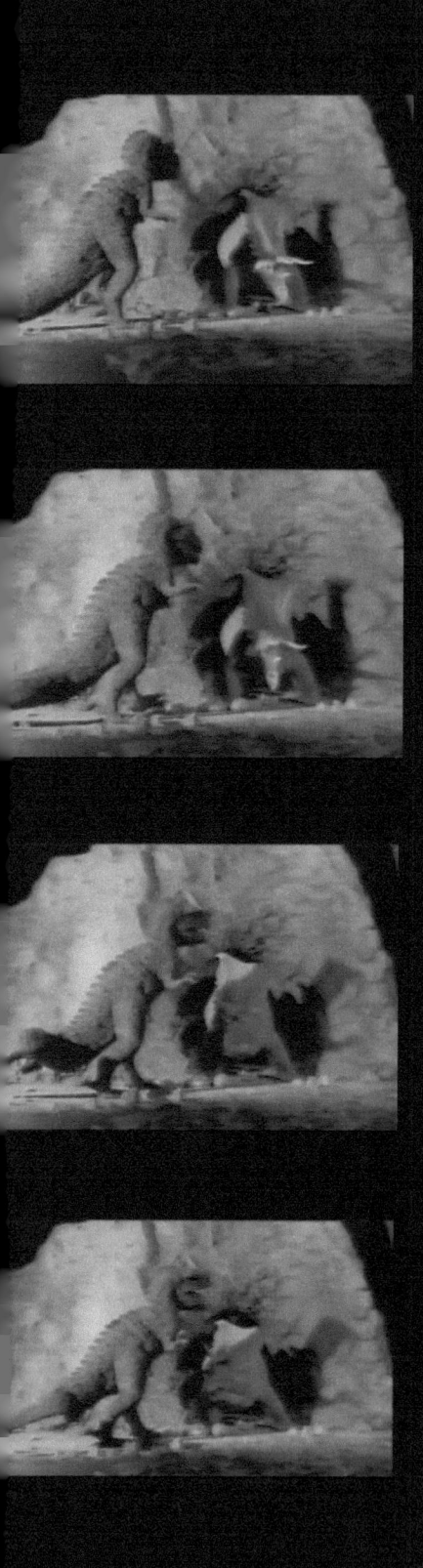

We've had a lot of trouble with water." [Ibid]

Hinds asked what kinds of ideas he had for the dinosaur picture. Since Ballard had yet to sign a contract or see any money he hadn't put much thought into it. According to him, he didn't even begin thinking of ideas until the car ride there! (A man after my own heart, doing his homework at the last second) Ballard outlined the ideas he thought up on the car ride over, though to my everlasting regret he doesn't say what those ideas were. Young and Hinds both agreed that his ideas were "Too original."

Hinds then went on to tell Ballard that they had already cooked up a story concept for the film. And, why bother to ask Ballard for ideas if they already had one? Presumably they wanted Ballard's name on the film and that was it. Ballard was bemused as Hinds went on to tell him that his secretary had come up with a story about the birth of the moon. Though poor Ballard often gets credited with the crazy idea, as you just read, it was not his idea after all. In Ballard's own words, he would never put such an idea on anyone's desk. Hinds looked into Ballard's eyes with a firm gaze and said, "We want you to tell us what happens next."

Ballard's own reminiscence on what happened next is just too funny to paraphrase, so here it is in his own words:

> I thought desperately, realizing that the film industry was not for me. 'A tidal wave?'
> 'Too many tidal waves. If you've seen one tidal wave you've seen them all.'
> A small light came on in the total darkness of my brain. 'But you always see the tidal waves coming in,' I said in a stronger

voice. 'We should show the tidal wave going out! All those strange creatures and plants...' I ended with a brief course in surrealist biology.

There was a silence as Hinds and Aida stared at each other. I assumed I was about to be shown the door.

'When the wave goes out...' Hinds stood up, clearly rejuvenated, standing behind his huge desk like Captain Ahab sighting the white whale. 'Brilliant. Jim, who's your agent?' [Ibid]

Ballard recalls that the trio went to dinner that night and talked about the characters and events that would appear in the film over fine wine. According to Ballard, soon after he wrote a treatment that was a bit different from the film, as evidenced by his comment that "some of [the treatment] survived into the finished film." [pp.228] When all was said and done, they misspelled Ballard's name in the film's opening credits! "As Hammer films go, it was a success, but I am glad that they misspelled my name in the credits," Ballard joked. [Ibid]

But, we're getting ahead of ourselves. The next step in the film's development was in securing a director in the form of Val Guest, who had helmed Hammer's first two Quartermass films. In June of 1968, Young traveled to Malta to approach a vacationing Guest (also the director of *Casino Royale* and *The Day the Earth Caught Fire* among others) about directing the picture. Guest, who thought a prehistoric adventure sounded fun, relates the episode in his memoir *So You Want to be in Pictures*. Guest asked, "How soon can I see the script?"

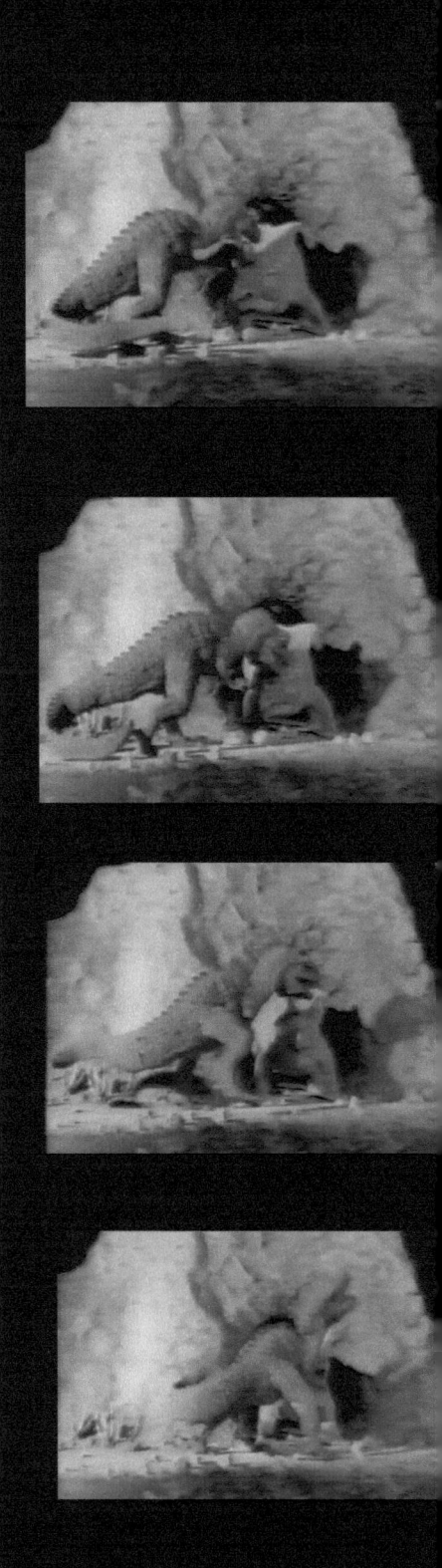

Above: *WDRTE's* two leads, Robin Hawdon as Tara and Victoria Vetri as Sanna. Inset: John Richardson as Tumak and Raquel Welch as Loana in *One Million Years B.C.* Something that Hawdon and Richardson both had in common was that both were considered for the role of James Bond. Richardson was eyed pre-*On Her Majesty's Secret Service* (1969), and Hawdon was offered an audition post-*Diamonds Are Forever* (1971).

Young burst into hysterics and replied, "You've got to be joking. The answer is: as soon as you finish writing it."

Guest spent the rest of his vacation writing the screenplay off of Ballard's rather short treatment. Considering that Guest claimed that he never saw *One Million Years B.C.*, and considering that *WDRTE* follows a very similar formula, then I would have to assume this means that Ballard's treatment must've followed the *B.C.* outline. As I wrote in the editorial, they have similar plotlines.

Back to Guest, he wanted to shoot the film in Malta. This would not only give it a different look from *B.C.*, but Guest could also stay at his vacation home there. But, thanks to tax incentives, Hammer returned to the Canary Islands where *B.C.* was shot, lending the sequel some visual continuity even if none of the actors were returning.

Pre-production poster advertising the film's production in 1968, along with another moon themed feature in the form of *Moon Zero Two* (which would coincidentally join *WDRTE* on its first U.S. DVD release as its double feature). Take note that many of the "in preparation" features on this poster never came to be, among them *In the Sun, When the World Cracked Open, The Reluctant Virgin, The Haunting of Toby Jugg, The Claw* and *Creatures the World Forgot* (not the same film released in 1971, see page 40 for the story on that).

Before production started the Hammer publicity machine was in full swing to promote their latest star discovery Victoria Vetri complete with a featurette entitled *Beauties and Beasts*. Vetri was handpicked by James Carreras himself, or so the feature claimed. Other sources say Young chose her while Guest claimed it was "someone in the American distributer's camp."

Whatever the case, Carreras said of her, "It's very difficult to be precise about what qualities of a girl catch my interest...I can't describe it but I know it when I see it, and Victoria Vetri has it I'm sure." The qualities that caught Carreras' eye were on full display in a 1967 issue of *Playboy* wherein Angela Dorian (aka Victoria Vetri) was that month's centerfold. Dorian was also Vetri's stage name that she went under in *Rosemary's Baby* wherein her character Terri is compared to "the actress Victoria Vetri" by Mia Farrow. By 1968 she went back to Vetri and was Playmate of the Year in addition to being Hammer's new star discovery.

Playing across from Vetri's character Sanna as her love interest Tara was Robin Hawdon, who had a role in Guest's *Day the Earth Caught Fire* and wrote plays in his spare time. Hawdon almost wasn't cast due to his youthful appearance. The *WDRTE* press book has a whole article on his casting process. He was turned away at first, which Hawdon wisely attributed to the

THE LOST FILMS FANZINE PRESENTS MOVIE MILESTONES #2

Jim Danforth consults with Victoria Vetri during shooting in the studio. Danforth's credit on the film was originally to read "Special Visual Effects Designed and Directed by" but the contract between the Director's Guild of America and Warner-Seven Arts forbade the use of the term "director" in conjunction with Danforth's part! Inset: Japanese magazine promoting the film.

fact that he was clean shaven. Wanting to get another shot at the role fast, he had a makeup man set him up with a fake beard. He wore that in front of Young and Guest, and got the job. Young remarked that she couldn't believe the difference the fake beard made, and Hawdon joked that he got the role "by a hair" in the *WDRTE* press book.

Hawdon elaborated on the incident in an interview with Richard Klemensen for *Little Shoppe of Horrors* #41. Hawdon reminisced thsat he read against an American bodybuilder named Hal Hamilton for the part. Guest apparently liked Hawdon's leaner look, but still instructed him to bulk up a bit for the part.

Two of the big creative forces behind the film: Aida Young and Jim Danforth (embarrassed to say I'm not sure who the man at far right is).

The next step was in finding a new special effects director, as Ray Harryhausen was already busy working on *The Valley of Gwangi*. Though Hammer debated on who to hire for several months, a few weeks before shooting began, they hired 28 year old Jim Danforth.

Hammer was smart enough to see to it that Danforth was also on location to advise Guest from what angles the dinosaurs (which he would animate later) would come in, etc. just as Harryhausen had done before him.

"It was relatively simple to shoot the picture," Guest told *Starlog Magazine* #163. "There was a very detailed storybook prepared—which I still have—showing where all the FX went in, shot by shot. All I did was follow that storybook."

["Inferno Maker Part II" by Steve Swires, pp.61]

Shooting went well aside from a few mishaps. And, despite many reports of Victoria Vetri being difficult to work with, Guest says nothing about that in his memoirs. Guest would seem to have more to say about Aida Young.

In an interview with Tom Weaver in his book *Attack of the Monster Movie Makers*, Guest implied that had it not been for Young he would've shot the picture differently. Guest wanted the movie to look like a TV documentary, as though you were really there in the prehistoric past. Rather than a cinematic look, he wanted a handheld camera look at times. He said, "...had I done it with Mike Carreras or even Tony Hinds, it would have been an entirely different picture... but [it was] just sort of another *One Million Years B.C.*"

21

Several rare photos of shooting the giant ant scene on location. From the Facebook Group "When Jim Danforth Ruled the Earth"

Several sequences were cut during shooting, some of them by Danforth himself because he knew they would take too long to animate, such as an ambitious pterodactyl hunt.

The most famous deleted scenes concerning *WDRTE* had a nest of giant Red Ants attacking the cave people during the scene where Kingsor's men chase down Tara and Sanna towards the end.

A smattering of shots filmed for this sequence made their way into the film, such as Sanna and Tara running through a charred, volcanic landscape.

The giant ant props were actually created, and some footage with them was shot. A stuntman was filmed wrestling with a three-foot-long ant armature. (Roger Dicken recalled to Mark Berry in *Dinosaur Filmography* that a local hotel proprietor wanted to buy the fiberglass prop to display in his bar!)

Shots were completed of a stuntman playing one of Kingsor's men running, staggering, and falling down with the three-foot-long prop strapped to his back. After he falls down, the idea was that six additional stopmotion ants would swarm his body. A stop motion puppet of the man would stand briefly only to fall back down until the ants consume him until nothing but a skeleton is left.

The ants would then turn their attention to Tara and Sanna, and chase them up a slope. Similar to *B.C.*'s axed brontosaur scene, the ants would be dispatched via magma. Tara would use his stone ax to breach an opening in the ground that spews out some lava, which would then run down and consume the ants.

The long shots of cavemen running in panic from the ants was shot too, in which Danforth would add the ants in later. Danforth recalled that Hammer wouldn't allow him use of the stuntmen in that scene for pay reasons, and so he had to use Spanish extras for those shots.

THE LOST FILMS FANZINE PRESENTS MOVIE MILESTONES #2

Left: Jim Danforth and the giant ant. Top right: Unused shot of the Rhamphorynchus. Danforth created an introduction for the beast that had it sitting atop a ledge during the dawn light. Hammer released a still of the shot, but that's it. Bottom right: Shot from the final film originally filmed in conjunction with the giant ant scene.

In his biography, *Dinosaurs, Dragons, and Drama*, Danforth recollects that he hired George Randle to do the ant armatures, of which there were six. According to Danforth, he saw the ants in the "new script" which would seem to imply they were a new addition to the story and weren't always there.

The ant sequence was one of the ones he tried to get Hammer to drop, but they were insistent upon it. "The ant sequence was on my list of sequences to be chopped, but they wouldn't accept that; they were really committed to having that particular sequence," Danforth said in *Photon* #20 when asked about it by Mark Frank.

To his relief, Hammer cut the scene in post-production to save time and money. Hammer didn't forget about the scene though, they scripted a similar scene in an unmade quasi-sequel, *When the Earth Cracked Open*. Also, the giant ants are still mentioned in the press book for *WDRTE*!

Another big deleted scene in—or rather not in—*WDRTE* was a pterosaur hunt, scripted by Guest, which, for whatever reason, Aida Young disliked. "Val had written a very nice pterodactyl sequence, in

Main image: Still from the wonderful Rhamphorynchus scene. Inset: Spanish release poster.

Guest did a second, less-complicated version of the scene that still did not please Young. "Val asked me to design something so I wrote a perfunctory pterodactyl sequence," Danforth said in *Lumier*. However, an alternate comment from Danforth to Mark Berry in *The Dinosaur Filmography* implies that Danforth himself felt the scene was too complicated to animate and would take too long. "It was a great sequence, but I just had to say, I can't do this for the time and budget that's available -- it's just too complicated," Danforth told Berry. [pp.419]

There were also a few non-existent deleted scenes from the film, which sprung from publicity photographs. To aid in the marketing, Hammer asked Danforth to work with a freelance still photographer on a few special

fact I thought it was the best sequence in the film. The producer threw it out, didn't like it," Danforth told Graham Shirley and Bill Taylor in *Lumiere* #25, in July of 1973.

The scene had one of the tribes out hunting for food. They come upon a pterodactyl nest and lower themselves down to it to steal some eggs. The two parents come along and eat some of the cavemen instead.

The film's ending was originally supposed to have more prehistoric creatures other than the giant crabs...

photographs of Vetri and the dinosaurs. The first photo had the mother dinosaur walking behind Vetri as she frolics naked in the wilderness. The image made its way into *Playboy* and also served as the basis of the Italian poster. The second image had a nude Vetri menaced by one of the giant crabs.

A great deal was cut from the climax, which would have been a prehistoric free for all. For instance, two pterodactyls were to attack the panicked cave people as the tidal wave loomed.

The live-action portion of the scene was shot as well, and possibly retained in the final cut. In this case, you might just think the actors were reacting to the storm, when in fact, it was invisible yet-to-be-added pterodactyls. As the film ran behind in post-production, it's not surprising this scene was cut.

Giant eels would have reared up from the sea too (which was to be accomplished by photographically enlarging real eels).

An article in *Monster Times* #40, entitled "Everything You Always Wanted to Know About Jim Danforth... but Didn't Know Where to Ask," claimed that the pterosaurs would meet their end being battered to death against some rocks. It also mentioned a "fight between two sea monsters" (presumably the eels), and a giant waterspout.

The ending sequence as a whole was particularly frustrating for Danforth because Young either couldn't or wouldn't give him a budget estimate for it. Therefore, Danforth didn't know if he could

Apparently, to save time, Warner Bros thought about giving Danforth a ten year old puppet of a baby dinosaur left over from *The Animal World* (1956)! This would have portrayed the famous baby dinosaur.

pull off all of his ideas or not. One ambitious shot he envisioned was to be a POV shot from atop the crest of the wave as though the theatergoers were riding it. After weeks and weeks of prep, when he delivered his ideas, Young informed them that they were too expensive (hence his wanting to know the budget!).

Another idea Danforth had was to build a miniature fiberglass tidal wave and tow it through the water while also spraying more water on it to obscure what it really was. Miniature rafts representing the escaping Sand People could be placed on the crest of the fiberglass wave, but that idea was tossed to the wayside too.

Four elaborate puppets were constructed to represent the film's heroes during the tidal wave scene. I get the impression there was supposed to be a shot of them riding the wave that had to be abandoned. Mark Berry's *Dinosaur Filmography*

reported that "The plan was to feature these puppets in a show-stopping miniature tidal wave sequence... but the sequence fell victim to financial belt-tightening." [pp.421]

Mark Wolf elaborated on the scene in his wonderful making of article in *Little Shoppe of Horrors* #41. Wolf confirmed the scene actually was shot, 18-inch puppets and all, on the Thames River, but was deemed unacceptable.

Ultimately Hammer would just use stock shots to create the tidal wave sequence.

The other alterations were minor, such as the mother dinosaur bringing a dead boar back to her nest rather than a deer. In another dropped idea, Guest wanted to Tara to cry at his dead friend's funeral barge, but Hawdon couldn't seem to muster any tears so the idea was dropped.

There was supposed to be a scene of Sanna, the baby dinosaur, and the mother all three frolicking together. Danforth storyboarded it, and I'm not sure if the live-action footage was shot or not and it was just the animation that was uncompleted.

After on location and studio shooting was over, Danforth's work began on the dinosaurs. Danforth said that while designing the dinosaurs, Hammer gave him a children's picture book. In some instances they wrote notes telling him to put one dinosaur' head on another's body! Danforth says that they eventually gave up on this method.

Famously, *WDRTE* technically only has one species of dinosaur: the Chasmosaurus. The rest technically qualify only as prehistoric reptiles (strange I know, but it's true). But, it almost had another: the T-Rex.

The reason for the T-Rex's excision was, of all things, the way the T-Rex carries its arms. Aida Young feared audiences would compare the dinosaur's stance to British homosexuals, at the time given the derogatory nickname of "poofs." Young even went so far as to comment she didn't want it to be nicknamed "poofsaurus."

The unused prop: Jim Danforth created a larger scale Tylosaur puppet that was apparently never used. This prop would've been more expensive to shoot due to difficulties with lighting and high speed photography. Also, there was an unused shot Danforth completed of the Tylosaur diving back under the water that Hammer didn't insert into the final cut for reasons unknown.

Roger Dicken did once dig out the old *Years B.C.* Allosaurus to have it battle the Chasmosaurus. It is sometimes mistaken for *WDRTE's* lost tyrannosaurus but it is not. It was actually test footage for a prehistoric flashback that went unused in *Trog* (1970). (Frames from the test footage can be seen on page 16-17)

Back to Young, she insisted that all the dinos be quadrupeds because she felt that all bipedal dinos looked effeminate! (This according to *Harryhausen: The Lost Movies*). It's thought that if this had not been the case, then perhaps the tyrannosaurus would have been the fearsome mother dinosaur. Instead a quadruped dinosaur in the vein of Harryhausen's classic *The Beast from 20,000 Fathoms* was created. Though, before that, an ankylosaur was considered and another early design had it looking more like a giant monitor lizard.

The Chasmosaurus was originally a Triceratops (Hammer's choice) until Danforth argued a new type of similar dinosaur be used since that variety had appeared in *B.C.* Next they suggested a styracosaurus, until Danforth informed Hammer that such a dinosaur was to appear in *Valley of Gwangi*. And so finally the Chasmosaurus was decided upon.

Ultimately, Danforth's work was positively stellar and even eclipsed that of his mentor Harryhausen (in my opinion). This is evidenced by the fact that *WDRTE* was nominated for an Academy Award for its effects work in 1971. Although it lost to *Bedknobs and Broomsticks*, it was still the only stop motion dinosaur film, or any type of Hammer production for that matter, to ever be nominated by the Academy. All in all Danforth's effects took 17 months to complete, finishing up in February 1970.

According to Val Guest, who was only able to partially edit the film, the final theatrical cut was quite different from what he had intended. Guest began editing work on the film with the primary editor, Peter Curran, before he found work on another project and moved on. A little while after that, Curran called him to tell him that, unfortunately, Aida Young had re-edited the picture in his absence. Guest claimed that he ultimately didn't even watch the film when it premiered. However, due to comments he made in *Hammer Horror* #7 he must've seen it eventually. He said that, "What went out on screen had nothing to do with the film I had made and left behind." [pp.25]

The film was released two years after principal photography had ended, on October 1, 1970. It did well enough for itself to land on *Kinematograph Weekly's* Top Money Makers List for that year. The film was released in the U.S. in March of 1971, running at 96 minutes (trimming out four minutes' worth of nude/sex scenes, but no dinosaur footage). Critics on neither side of the Atlantic were kind to it, but that didn't matter. The film made a profit, and that, as always, was the bottom line.

"WHEN DINOSAURS RULED THE EARTH"

NOMINATED FOR: BEST ACHIEVEMENT IN VISUAL EFFECTS (JIM DANFORTH)

Above: Ad for *WDRTE*'s nomination for Best Effects. Below: The mother dinosaur as it appeared in *WDRTE*. After this, Danforth refitted the armature to become a brand new monster, the Dyrrth, from his aborted production of *At the Earth's Core*.

THE LOST U-CUT THAT ALMOST WAS

As I stated in the editorial, *WDRTE* was released in the U.S. in a G-Rated cut sans two major nude scenes. In early April of 1973, Hammer was thinking or rereleasing the film under the U.K. equivalent of the G Rating, called the U Certificate. Though this would never come to pass, on April 2, 1973, the censors set forth several recommendations that concerned everything but the nudity!

Their first suggestion was to trim the plesiosaur's graphic death, specifically to remove its head being on fire and its howls of pain. They wanted the fight between Sanna and Ayak trimmed, but didn't specify how (notably they didn't call for its excision altogether though).

The caveman who got killed by the giant snake needed to go, and the scene of the man-eating plant trying to eat Sanna needed to be removed altogether.

The censors wanted Tara's fight with the pterodactyl trimmed, specifically the removal of close-ups. They also wanted close-ups of Tara in pain as he's given a live funeral barge removed.

The last recommended cut was to trim violence from the giant crab attack. As you can see, there's no mention at all about the nude scenes (unless those went without saying). It's rather hilarious that all the suggested cuts above were in the U.S. G rated version with no trimming at all! Essentially, while the British board abhorred the violence, the U.S. board was only timid about the nudity.

Above: Super 8mm versions of *WDRTE* and *B.C.* Below: The plesiosaurs scene from *WDRTE* was possibly inspired by a cancelled scene involving a brontosaurs from *B.C.* where it was to have attacked the Rock Tribe.

FROM Warner bros. A Kinney company
PRESSBOOK

'WHEN DINOSAURS RULED THE EARTH' BOASTS BLONDE BEAUTIES, TRIBAL WARS, REPTILES

Victoria Vetri in Debut Hawdon Has Male Lead

"When Dinosaurs Ruled the Earth," a Warner Bros. prehistoric drama opening in Technicolor on . . . . at the . . . . . Theatre, fills the screen with tribal wars, a near human sacrifice to the sun god, a climactic tidal wave and very possibly filmdom's next top sex symbol in the person of California beauty Victoria Vetri.

Voluptuous (37-21-35) Victoria, named *Playboy Magazine's* "Playmate of the Year" in 1968, headlines the cast as Sanna, the world's first blonde who narrowly avoids becoming a human sacrifice to the gods. Robin Hawdon has the male lead as her protector.

Appearing with them are Patrick Allen, Sean Caffrey, Imogen Hassall and Magda Konopka.

Producer Aida Young and director Val Guest have brought to the prehistoric drama both a sense of fun and a studied authenticity and sense of realism not often found in the films of the "prehistoric" genre.

Both producer and director set out to prove wrong the dictum that every "dinosaur picture" is the same. Guest, in particular, believed that it was possible and desirable to employ a "new documentary" treatment of the subject and still maintain the film's primary task of entertaining a vast audience.

Guest describes his own screenplay as "science-fact" as opposed to "science-fiction" because evidence uncovered from the past permits the telling of "fact" films whereas science-fiction depends upon guesswork about the future.

The realistic film style is attributed, in part, to the director of animation, James Danforth, who spent one year creating giant reptiles, an authentic-looking moon, a tidal wave and an invasion of giant crabs.

Other key unit men included director of photography Dick Bush, assistant director John Stoneman, sound recordist Kevin Sutton and musical composer Mario Nascimbene.

Guest assigned two choreographers from London's famed Royal Ballet Company to stage a wild tribal dance, and several London linguists to invent a primitive 27-word language.

MARIE O'BRIEN is sacrificed to the sun god in Warner Bros. "When Dinosaurs Ruled the Earth," the prehistoric drama starring Victoria Vetri and Robin Hawdon, which opens in Technicolor on ___ at the ___ Theatre.

Mat 1-A   Still No. 30016-7

Here ROBIN HAWDON challenges tribal leader PATRICK ALLEN in "When Dinosaurs Ruled the Earth," the Warner Bros. prehistoric drama opening in Technicolor on ___ at the ___ Theatre. Directed by Val Guest, the film headlines the blonde beauty Victoria Vetri.

Mat 2-C   Still No. 30016-15

Victoria Vetri Joins Dinosuars To Make Noticeable Film Debut

Voluptuous Victoria Vetri is the latest in a glittering line of sex goddesses from the company that launched such international screen beauties as Ursula Andress, Raquel Welch and Olinka Berova.

Victoria makes her starring debut as Sanna, the world's first blonde in "When Dinosaurs Ruled the Earth," the prehistoric drama made by Hammer Films for Warner Bros.' which opens in color on . . . . . at the . . . . . Theatre.

Miss Vetri headlines the cast with Robin Hawdon, Patrick Allen, Drewe Henley, Sean Caffrey and Magda Konopka. Val Guest directed his own screenplay on locations in the Canary Islands and at the Shepperton Studios in England. Aida Young produced the film.

It was Mrs. Young who was attracted to Victoria when she noticed the photographic layout in Playboy Magazine naming Victoria, then known as Angela Dorian, the "Playmate of the Year" in 1968.

"I guess she thought I looked lean and hungry like a prehistoric female savage," the young actress explains. "In the picture I'm not really savage, though. There are tender scenes which show that even early men and women had the ability to express finer emotions."

The gorgeous California blonde pulls no punches when she talks about her role as a sex symbol of the screen. "In 'Dinosaurs' I appear in the nude for two love scenes. One takes place in a cave and the other in the sea. I don't object to them because I realize that this opportunity to make an impact in films is so important to me that I'm not about to forfeit it out of silly prudery."

Victoria has many moments in which to display her impressive measurements (37-21-35) to best advantage in the prehistoric-styled bikini outfits she and the other young beauties wear on screen.

Apart from her acting ability, Victoria is a keen athlete and a dedicated sun worshipper. Equally at home on water skis, ballet tights or skin-diving dress (she maintains her own diving tank at her California home), the sultry blonde notes that she became a sun-worshipper "when I discovered that in astrology and even in mythology, the sun is regarded as the masculine planet."

One day, Miss Vetri hopes to develop into a first-rate dramatic actress. In the meantime, she is grateful that "When Dinosaurs Ruled the Earth" gives her the all-important chance for wide recognition. And it's safe to say—she will be noticed.

Blonde VICTORIA VETRI and ROBIN HAWDON, romantic members of rival tribes, are the world's first Romeo and Juliet in Warner Bros. Technicolor prehistoric drama, "When Dinosaurs Ruled the Earth," opening on ___ at the ___ Theatre.

Mat 1-B   Still No. 30016-56
Special Publicity Still

ROBIN HAWDON, who stars with Victoria Vetri, battles a sea monster in the prehistoric drama from Warner Bros., "When Dinosaurs Ruled the Earth," opening in Technicolor on ___ at the ___ Theatre. Val Guest directed his own screenplay in the Canary Islands and in England.

Mat 2-A   Still No. 30016-3

Dinosaur Film Opens Today

Tribal warfare, prehistoric monsters, a climactic tidal wave and one of the world's great beauties, Victoria Vetri, bring excitement to the silver screen starting today at the . . . . . Theatre in Warner Bros.' prehistoric drama, "When Dinosaurs Ruled the Earth."

Produced by Aida Young and directed by Val Guest, who wrote his own screenplay, "When Dinosaurs Ruled the Earth" was shot on locations in the Canary Islands and in England. Robin Hawdon has the male lead.

Robin's Career Had Close Shave Improved by Not Shaving At All

Robin Hawdon is one actor who got his big break without a close shave.

His story began several years ago when he appeared briefly in Val Guest's award-winning science-fiction drama, "The Day the Earth Caught Fire."

When Hawdon later heard that Guest was to direct Warner Bros.' "When Dinosaurs Ruled the Earth," the prehistoric drama opening on . . . . . at the . . . . . Theatre, the young actor arranged to be interviewed by both Guest and producer Aida Young for the male lead.

Unknown to Robin, Val Guest, impressed with Robin's previous work, had seriously considered starring him opposite the voluptuous newcomer Veronica Vetri.

"But, in the end, I was off the list because I was too young-looking," admits the actor whose youthful appearance belies his actual age of 30. "They needed a fairly mature type to help Veronica fight those prehistoric monsters and bloodthirsty cavemen."

Having read the script, Robin was determined to play the hero. He persuaded a make-up man to loan him a false beard and arranged a second meeting with the director and producer.

"When he walked in wearing that beard," Aida recalls, "he seemed so right I couldn't believe that a small fringe of hair could make so much difference."

"You might say I got the role by a hair," Robin jokes.

Robin, a graduate of England's Royal Academy of Dramatic Arts, has appeared on stage with several of England's top thespian talents including Sir John Geilgud, Sir Ralph Richardson and Anna Massey. He first starred in "The Easter Man" in London's West End.

Hawdon is equally talented as a playright with four completed plays to his credit.

A fearsome prehistoric creature provides plenty of thrills and excitement in Warner Bros.' "When Dinosaurs Ruled the Earth," which opens in Technicolor on ___ at the ___ Theatre. Victoria Vetri and Robin Hawdon star in the drama directed by Val Guest.

Mat 2-F   Still No. 30016-90   (Special Publicity Still)

'Voice-Over' King Turns Demagogue

Patrick Allen describes the role that carries him from TV commercials to large-scale screen success as "a demagogue in loincloth."

His is one of the featured roles in Warner Bros.' prehistoric drama starring sex goddess Victoria Vetri and Robin Hawdon titled "When Dinosaurs Ruled the Earth," opening on . . . . . at the . . . . . Theatre.

"Despite his evilness, the demagogue Kingsor is worthy of sympathy," Allen feels. "The able tribal leader is motivated by fear and superstition because he really believes that unless the world's first blonde is offered as a sacrifice to the gods his people will be punished."

Allen, known as the "king of the voice-overs" in an England full of superb elocutionists was so much in demand as a commercial's narrator that even while he was filming "When Dinosaurs Ruled the Earth" on location in the Canary Islands he was required to spend several lunch hours recording commercials.

© 1970 Warner Bros. Inc.

Val Guest Writes New Language For Actors in 'Dinosaurs' Film

"We have taken one large liberty for the sake of narrative fun" explains Val Guest, the writer and director of Warner Bros.' prehistoric drama, "When Dinosaurs Ruled the Earth," opening in color on _____ at the _____ Theatre. "We have dinosaurs, which in fact were extinct before human beings evolved, on the same screen with men and women. But aside from that we played it by the book."

The entire film—from cave decor to costumes—was founded on months of research about the prehistoric era in British museums. One of the most fascinating aspects of Guest's scholarly approach was the creation of an exclusive 27-word language developed from a mixture of ancient Phoenician, Latin and Sanskrit tongues.

"The words are not merely arbitrary sounds. The word for killing is a sharp one—*N'kan*—as the act itself implies. And our word for gone has no relation to Ringo Starr's son of the same name, *Zak*," Guest advises.

"Learning the film language was like being a tourist in a foreign country where you know only four or five guide-book words," says voluptuous and sexy Victoria Vetri. "There are less words in 'Dinosaurs' than in my short appearance in the laundry room scene with Mia Farrow in 'Rosemary's Baby,'" the star observes.

"This isn't a word film," Guest is quick to point out. "The minimal use of dialogue forced me to think in the style of the silent cinema directors. The emphasis is on the visuals and the action."

And there is plenty of action on the widescreen at the birth of the Moon, a pterodactyl attack, a tidal wave and an all-for-fun sequence in which Miss Vetri is adopted by a dinosaur is depicted.

PATRICK ALLEN, leader of the Rock Tribe, exhorts his people to action in Warner Bros.' "When Dinosaurs Ruled the Earth," opening in Technicolor on _____ at the _____ Theatre.

Mat 1-C Still No. 30016-634

'JUST A HOUSEWIFE' PRODUCES FILMS LAUNCHES STARS

Aida Young says she is "just a Hampstead housewife and mother of two daughters." But she is also one of the world's half-dozen successful women film producers.

In keeping with her specialty of producing adventure, mystery and science-fiction films, Mrs. Young's latest project for Warner Bros. is "When Dinosaurs Ruled the Earth," opening on _____ at the _____ Theatre.

"The film, starring voluptuous Victoria Vetri and Robin Hawdon, is real cinema, like the old silent days—entertaining, imaginative and almost historical," she explains.

Mrs. Young has been involved in filmmaking for more than 25 years. She got her start during the Second World War at a time when manpower was in critical shortage. She admits that being a woman has made it more difficult to fight for equal acceptance, but that she learned the business from the ground up has always held her in good stead.

To prepare herself for the production of her first horror film, Warner Bros.' "Dracula Has Risen from the Grave," Aida watched six horror films in a row. "I'd never seen a horror film in my life and I staggered out into the sunshine feeling quite sick and terrified after they were all over." Now she enjoys the medium very much.

As associate producer of "She" and "One Million Years B.C." and full producer of "The Vengeance of She" Aida is personally credited with introducing such glamorous stars as Raquel Welch, Ursula Andress and Olinka Berova to the screen.

Funeral rites for DREWE HENLEY are held as MAGDA KONOPKA looks on in Warner Bros.' prehistoric drama, "When Dinosaurs Ruled the Earth," the Victoria Vetri and Robin Hawdon starrer which opens in Technicolor on _____ at the _____ Theatre. Val Guest was the director.

Mat 2-B Still No. 30016-2

HAPPY ENDING IN DINOSAURS

Warner Bros.' "When Dinosaurs Ruled the Earth," opening in color on _____ at the _____ Theatre, might well be described as a prehistoric "Romeo and Juliet."

The romantic leads, played by voluptuous Victoria Vetri and Robin Hawdon, cannot claim to be of the houses of Montague or Capulet, but they are members of the opposing Rock and Shell tribes.

As such, hero Tara must decide between his allegiance to the superstitious tribesmen who plan to sacrifice blonde heroine Sanna, to a sun god or to go against his people and help her escape.

One major difference between Shakespeare's renowned play and director Guest's screenplay is that "When Dinosaurs Ruled the Earth" ends on a much happier note.

'KING KONG' CAUGHT DANFORTH FOR LIFE

Jim Danforth went to see the film classic "King Kong" when he was 12 years old. "I didn't believe that the giant was 50 feet tall, but I wasn't terrified," he recalls. "I knew there was a trick and that was what fascinated me." So he went home and set about discovering how the trick was done.

16 years of investigation and valuable experience in films and TV more than qualified Jim, at age 28, to tackle the special visual effects seen in Warner Bros.' prehistoric drama, "When Dinosaurs Ruled the Earth," opening on _____ at the _____ Theatre.

Among his various assignments, Jim created an exciting astronaut's view of the Moon as it originally parted company with the Sun. He also made a playful dinosaur which reminded him of his first professional animation project involving a rabbit who danced on TV with Dinah Shore.

In addition to all the dinosaurs and pterodactyls, "When Dinosaurs Ruled the Earth" stars blonde beauty Victoria Vetri and Robin Hawdon. Val Guest directed his own screenplay.

VICTORIA VETRI, captured here by PATRICK ALLEN and chief hunter BILLY CORNELIUS, has more serious problems to contend with as a dinosaur approaches in Warner Bros.' prehistoric drama, "When Dinosaurs Ruled the Earth," opening in Technicolor on _____ at the _____ Theatre.

Mat 2-D Still No. 30016-77
Special Publicity Still

the story

A fiery ball breaks away from the Sun, giving birth to the Moon. Awed, a primitive Rock Tribe blame the resulting upheaval of the Earth's surface on fair-haired Sanna (VICTORIA VETRI) and condemns her to death.

Escaping from the sacrificial ceremony, the maiden is blown into the sea by a cyclone, then rescued by Tara (ROBIN HAWDON), a bronzed rugged apprentice fisherman of the neighbouring Sand Tribe. Sanna, however, incites a girl called Ayak (IMOGEN HASSALL) to jealousy, for she considers Tara her property.

Soon, Sanna must flee again after Kingsor (PATRICK ALLEN), chief of the Rock Tribe, arrives to explain that her affront to the Sun has caused the new fire in the sky. Encountering monsters, a snake and a man-eating plant, Sanna finally takes refuge in the nest of a dinosaur, and is accepted as one of its young. For a while, she lives among the dinosaurs.

Tara, in pursuit, finds Sanna's hair in the deadly plant and gives her up for lost. Homeward bound, he saves a wounded warrior of the Rock Tribe, Kane (SEAN CAFFREY), from a triceratops, and takes him back to the Sand Tribe to be tended by Ulido (MAGDA KONOPKA), whose husband was killed by the monster.

After Kane has recovered from his injuries, Tara helps him return to the Rock Tribe. On his way home, Tara sees, in the valley below, Sanna being pursued by a huge dinosaur. Running to save her, he discovers they are playing. Now, Sanna and Tara spend their first peaceful moments in the cave where she lives.

Unfortunately, Sanna's romp with the dinosaur was witnessed by a member of the Rock Tribe. When Tara returns home, he finds that Kingsor has visited the Sand Tribe and inflamed them against him. Refusing to divulge where Sanna is, Tara is bound and set adrift on a blazing raft.

He escapes, but in helping Sanna elude an army of giant ants—as well as the men who are searching for her—Tara is re-captured. As Tara is about to be burned at the stake on the beach, the gravitational pull of the Moon causes the Earth's first tide.

A monster wave now sweeps inland, carrying everything before it. Sanna arrives in time to save Tara, and with the aid of Kane and Ulido, they fight their way to a raft. When they finally reach, their enemies are all dead. As the quartet face the new, uncharted world, the moon clears, bathing them in its radiant glow.

running time 96 minutes

cast

VICTORIA VETRI	Sanna
ROBIN HAWDON	Tara
PATRICK ALLEN	Kingsor
DREWE HENLEY	Khaku
SEAN CAFFREY	Kane
MAGDA KONOPKA	Ulido
IMOGEN HASSALL	Ayak
PATRICK HOLT	Ammon
JAN ROSSINI	Rock Girl
CAROL-ANNE HAWKINS	Yani
MARIA O'BRIEN	Omah
CONNIE TILTON	Sand Mother
MAGGIE LYNTON	Rock Mother
JIMMY LODGE	Fisherman
BILLY CORNELIUS	Hunter
RAY FORD	Hunter

credits

Director, Val Guest; Producer, Aida Young; Screenplay, Val Guest; Treatment, J.B. Ballard; Director of Photography, Dick Bush; Art Director, John Blezard; Editor, Peter Curran; Special Effects, Allan Bryce, Roger Dicken, Brian Johncock; Sound Recordist, Kevin Sutton; Special Visual Effects, Jim Danforth; Music Composer & Special Music Effects, Mario Nascimbene; Musical Supervision, Philip Martell; Production Manager, Christopher Sutton; Costume Designer, Carl Toms; 2nd Unit Camera, Johnny Cabrera; 2nd Unit Continuity, Susana Merry; Makeup Supervisor, Richard Mills; Hairdressing Supervisor, Joyce James; Wardrobe Master, Brian Owen-Smith; Construction Manager, Albert Blackshaw; Continuity, Josephina Knowles; Assistant Director, John Stoneman.

billing

Warner Bros. presents	25%
A Hammer Film Production	25%
WHEN DINOSAURS RULED THE EARTH	100%
Starring	
VICTORIA VETRI	100%
ROBIN HAWDON	50%
PATRICK ALLEN	50%
IMOGEN HASSALL	50%
Music Composed by Mario Nascimbene	10%
Special Visual Effects Jim Danforth	15%
Written for the Screen by Val Guest	15%
Technicolor (R)	15%
Produced by Aida Young	15%
Directed by Val Guest	15%
Distributed by Warner Bros.	

FOUR PAGE CAVEMANS DICTIONARY

This exciting Caveman's Dictionary is available to showmen for their engagement of "When Dinosaurs Ruled the Earth." Hand them out through co-operating stores and to theatre patrons several weeks in advance of your booking.

To make the fullest use of the Dictionaries use the Caveman language as the basis for contests and teaser ads in newspapers, both on the theatre page and in the classified columns. These Ads could read "AKHOBA OSORS TEDAKS N'DYE (phone number)" when interested people call they get the translation ("Help, Dinosaurs and Flying Monsters are coming"), as well as your playdate, on a recorded message. Only a limited number of these promotion pieces are available so order today from Mr. Leo Wilder, Warner Bros., 4000 Warner Blvd., Burbank, Calif. 91505

Mr. Exhibitor,

The "Dinosaurs" coloring mat is an important and valuable promotion aid for your campaign. The four-column mat, including the impressive artwork title (not shown) is available FREE. Order it well in advance or print directly from this illustration and insert the title from Ad Mat 203. Many people, both young and old, enjoy coloring and the response should be rewarding.

This mat contest gives you innumerable opportunities for tie-ups with local merchants. Promote prizes from them and allow them to distribute blanks to their customers. Order the free mat from:
CAMPAIGN PLAN MANAGER
Warner Bros. Studios
4000 Warner Blvd.
Burbank, Calif. 91505

Sample copy for mat

To enter the "When Dinosaurs Ruled the Earth" coloring contest, just complete the picture and bring it to the Theatre. You can use crayons, water colors or pastels. Winners will be announced. All entries must be received no later than

Fight Dinosaurs Three Ways With Four-Color Door Panels

Three Beautiful Girls Will Work For You

Let everybody in town know "Dinosaurs" is coming to your theatre with vivid two-color door panels featuring buxom beauties battling ferocious, scaly monsters. Let these beautiful girls work for you — they'll certainly call attention to your engagement. There is no particular sequence for the placement of the four door panels. Send for them soon.

Order from:
Campaign Plan Manager, Warner Bros. Studios
4000 Warner Blvd., Burbank, Calif. 91505

Teaser Trailers

The birth of the moon — primitive tribal sacrifice — a beautiful woman who could tame any man — unimaginable dangers from monstrous reptiles — these thrilling scenes from "When Dinosaurs Ruled The Earth" are captured in the colorful trailers now ready for your campaign. Screen the spectacular production trailer often for best results, and use the teaser trailer for crossplugging in your own and other theatres.

Order now from: Order from National Screen Service.

TV Excerpt

Your audience will be awed by the terrors of the primeval world — the great reptilian beasts challenged by savage man — the tribal fear and feminine beauty that pervade "When Dinosaurs Ruled The Earth." The colorful excerpt is adaptable for use on talk shows, in your lobby, and after TV movies.

Order now from:
CAMPAIGN PLAN MANAGER
Warner Bros., 400 Warner Blvd.
Burbank, Calif. 91505

Radio Spots

From the creators of "One Million BC" comes their most gigantic spectacle — "When Dinosaurs Ruled the Earth." That's what your listeners will hear when you use these free radio spots — 60-seconds, 20-seconds and 10-seconds long — to tell them about the film's violent prehistoric drama and Victoria Vetri's provocative role as the world's first blonde. Order now from:

Eugene Gromek, Suski Productions, 165 W. 46th St., New York, N.Y. 10036

TV Spots

Take your customers back to the very beginning of time before man became master — when terror, superstition and primeval monsters ruled the world — with the five FREE TV spots available for your campaign. Full of action-color-excitement-the spots come in 60-second, 30-second, two 20-second and 10-second lengths. Write for them today from:

Campaign Plan Manager, Warner Bros. Studios
4000 Warner Blvd., Burbank, Calif. 91505

Featurette

In this colorful featurette, your patrons will see Sir James Carreras discovering the beautiful women who star in his films. They'll recall the faces and figures of his former finds, including Raquel Welch and Ursula Andress, always surrounded by massive, primeval monsters. And they'll be introduced to "Dinosaurs'" star Victoria Vetri, Sir James' latest addition to a thrilling tradition of ill-clad beauties facing giant reptiles. The making of this star of luscious proportions is the making of a fascinating film subject. Request from:

Mr. Leo Wilder, Warner Bros. Studios
4000 Warner Blvd., Burbank, Calif. 91505

NOTE: For our records, please include the name and call letters of station on which they will be used.

Lobby Record

The unique primordial sounds from "Dinosaurs" — the grunts of primitive savages, the shrieks of women, the bone-crushing jaws and gnashing teeth of monsters — are combined on the free Lobby Record prepared for your campaign. Appropriate sell copy, interspersed with the extraordinary sound effects, will draw customers into your theatre. Be sure to order the record right away, and plan to play it in your lobby both before and during your engagement.

Contact:
Eugene Gromek, Suski Productions
165 W. 46th Street, New York, N.Y. 10036

2 Col. x 99 lines = 198 lines   Mat No. 204

2 Col. x 49 lines = 98 lines   Mat No. 203

All advertising in this pressbook, as well as all other advertising and publicity materials referred to herein, has been approved under the standards for Advertising of the Code of Self-Regulation of the Motion Picture Association of America. All inquiries on this procedure may be addressed to:
Director of the Code for Advertising
Motion Picture Association of America
522 Fifth Avenue, New York, N.Y. 10036
This picture has been rated:

ACCESSORIES AVAILABLE FROM N.S.S.

BIG HI-RISE STANDEE is a major exploitation item. Its actual size is 40 x 60 and the cost is only $9.95, plus a one-time charge of $1.50 for the re-usable pole and stand.

---ALSO---

The 24 x 82 Title Display comes in brilliant Da-Glo colors. It is available on a rental basis — contact your local N.S.S. Exchange Manager for information and rates.

3 Col. x 98 lines = 294 lines   Mat No. 301

2 Col. x 28 lines = 56 lines   Mat No. 202

1 Col. x 71 lines   Mat No. 102

2 Col. x 15 lines = 30 lines   Mat No. 201

1 Col. x 14 lines   Mat. No. 101

```
COMBINATION
AD-PUB MAT
Includes Ad Mats
  101    102
  201    203
And Scene Cuts
 1-B   2-D   2-F
```

4 Col. x 123 lines = 492 lines   Mat No. 401

Posters and Accessories
also available : ★ 12 color 8 x 10's ★ 8 color 11 x 14's

Six Sheet

22 x 28

14 x 36

One Sheet

Three Sheet

This special 40 x 60 based on the popular CAVEMAN'S DICTIONARY is available on a limited basis. Use this selling feature to promote word contests and in connection with teaser ads. A limited supply of this special poster is available free from:

Mr. Leo Wilder
WARNER BROS.
4000 Warner Blvd.
Burbank, California 91505

Printed in U.S.A.

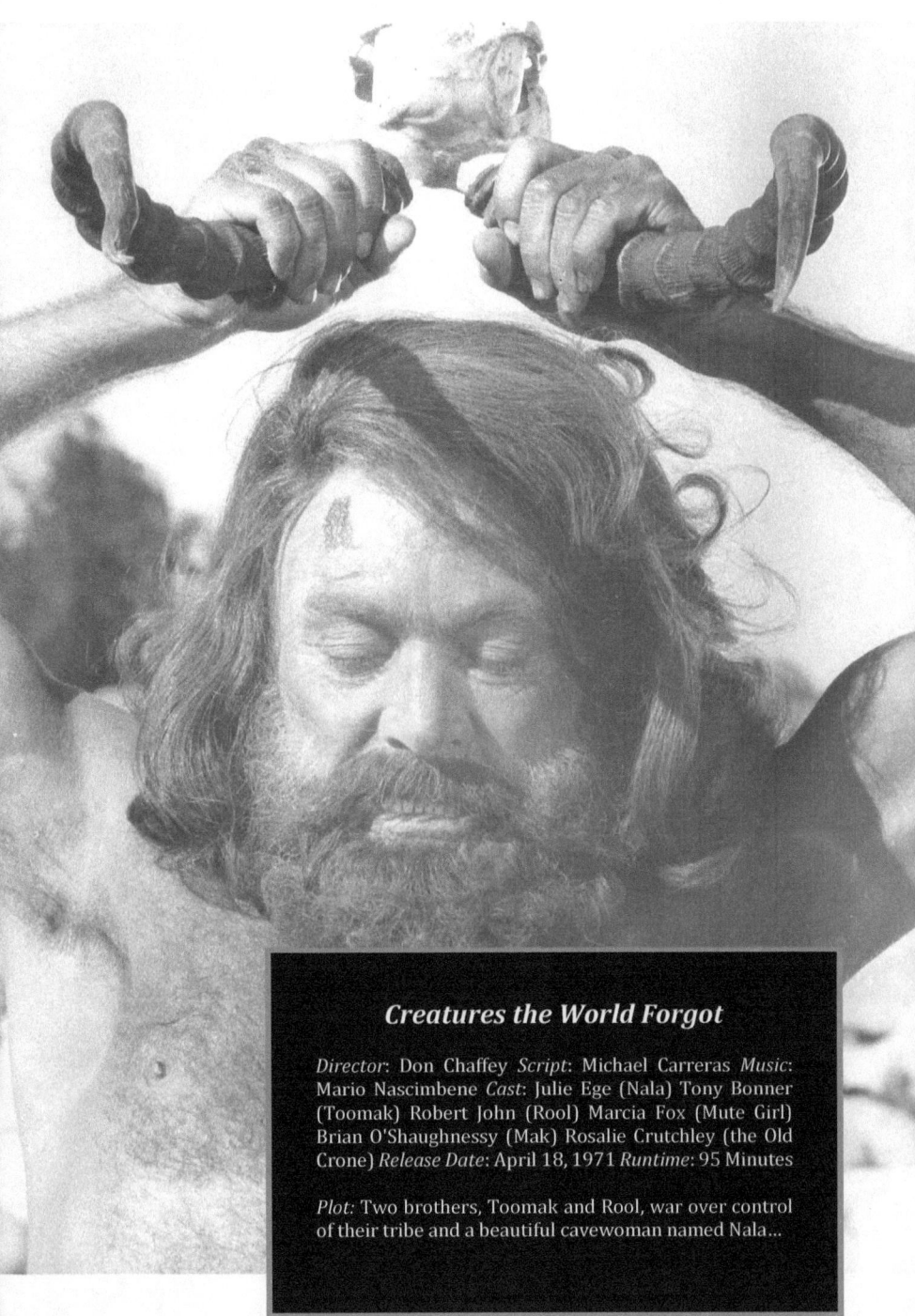

Creatures the World Forgot

Director: Don Chaffey *Script*: Michael Carreras *Music*: Mario Nascimbene *Cast*: Julie Ege (Nala) Tony Bonner (Toomak) Robert John (Rool) Marcia Fox (Mute Girl) Brian O'Shaughnessy (Mak) Rosalie Crutchley (the Old Crone) *Release Date*: April 18, 1971 *Runtime*: 95 Minutes

Plot: Two brothers, Toomak and Rool, war over control of their tribe and a beautiful cavewoman named Nala...

SEQUELS THAT THE WORLD FORGOT

AND HOW ZEPPELIN V PTERODACTYLS TURNED INTO CREATURES THE WORLD FORGOT

As had been the case with *B.C.*, *WDRTE* inspired several unfinished projects and also one sequel, 1971's *Creatures the World Forgot*. Most of the proposed follow-ups were pitched before *WDRTE* had even finished post-production. Many of these projects weren't really sequels so much as they were fantasy films featuring dinosaurs.

If you'll recall, Hammer had wanted to remake *King Kong* before remaking *One Million B.C.* RKO had denied Hammer the rights to a remake, and said they would only license the character for sequels. After the release of *WDRTE*, Hammer decided to try again. So confident were they that they even advertised that they would be doing the remake before they had secured RKO's permission!

The plan was probably to re-use some of the dinosaur models from *WDRTE* in the Kong remake, but that's just my conjecture. Hammer approached Ray Harryhausen about the possibility of doing the effects, and, while he wasn't wild about the idea of a remake, he figured if it was going to be done he might as well be the one to do it. Once again, RKO denied Hammer remake rights (even though they would change their mind only a few years later when both Universal and Dino De Laurentiis launched competing remakes).

The aborted Hammer Kong remake did lead to a funny King Kong Volkswagen commercial, though. David Allen, one of the animators on *WDRTE*, became so excited by the prospect that he shot color test footage of Kong atop the Empire State Building. He used the footage in his portfolio, and was eventually hired by an advertising firm on a commercial utilizing Kong to promote the new VW superbug.

Jim Danforth (left) with *WDRTE's* Chasmosaurus and David Allen (right) with his King Kong, which sadly never got to star in a Hammer remake as planned.

The commercial aired in 1972. It was wildly popular with audiences, but VW executives loathed it, feeling it either distracted from the car or provided false advertising—as though anyone really believed the car was as big as Kong...

While the Kong remake was only tangentially related to *WDRTE*, there were plans for a direct sequel. All we really know about it is that it was called *Dinosaur Girl*. There's nothing really concrete about it other than multiple sources all say the same thing about it, which is that it was to continue the adventures of Sanna and her baby dinosaur.

Now, back in those days, that didn't necessarily mean that Vetri would return to the role. Knowing Hammer, they would've simply cast another blonde who was cheaper and went on their way à la *Vengeance of She*. As to other little details, some forums stated that Jim Danforth claimed the follow-up would be a comedy of sorts, though we can't find anything concrete on that comment. Many sources claim Hammer dropped *Dinosaur Girl* due to the lengthy nature of stopmotion. But this doesn't gel with the fact that, around the same time, Hammer was flirting with another dinosaur concept. This one would have eschewed the cavepeople to a degree and was called *Lost Creations*.

The project didn't start at Hammer. It was an independent project by David Allen and Dennis Muren that began gestating in 1967. Jim Danforth was brought into the fold, and the title changed to *Raiders of the Stone Ring*. And thus begins the long winding, intertwining road of *Creatures the World Forgot* and *The Primevals*...

During *WDRTE*'s production, someone, possibly Jim Danforth, reportedly pitched to Hammer an adaptation of Edgar Rice Burroughs' *The Land That Time Forgot*. That idea lasted nary a second, when someone at Hammer realized it would be cheaper to do a similar type of story without having to pay the Burrough's estate, which tied in perfectly with Allen and Muren's current story. *TLTTF* would eventually be produced by Hammer's main rival, Amicus, a few years later.

Allen was the main creative force in terms of writing, and concocted something quite similar to *The Land That Time Forgot*. He lacked a proper third act, however, and Danforth suggested that they deviate from Burroughs to H.G. Wells. Danforth apparently was the one who suggested a race of lizard men similar to the Morlocks of *The Time Machine*.

From what I can tell, and I could very well be wrong, it was Danforth who provided the connection to Hammer. A treatment entitled *Zeppelins vs. Pterodactyls* was submitted to Hammer in June of 1970, shortly before *WDRTE*'s release.

Set shortly after WWI rather than during it, as was the case in the Burroughs story, *ZvP* concerned an anthropologist named Edward Fulmer seeking an ancient civilization in the Arctic (inspired by the original *She* novel, perhaps?). Twenty years earlier, Fulmer's mentor, Richard Hayward, had disappeared in the Arctic searching for the lost city. Fulmer's party travels by zeppelin and finds Hayward's ship stuck in the ice.

The dirigible eventually comes across a Caprona-like tropical oasis surrounded by walls of ice. Similar to *The People that Tome Forgot* (the novel and the 1977 film alike), the airship is attacked by pterodactyls. The heroes pilot a biplane to counter the creatures, but tears in the balloon force the zeppelin to land in the prehistoric land.

The plane is forced to crash-land too. In it were Fulmer and a reporter named Gordon Easton. Separated from the dirigible (this is similar now to *Tarzan at the Earth's Core*), the two must trek the mysterious land on foot. The first creature they encounter on land is a

THE LOST FILMS FANZINE PRESENTS MOVIE MILESTONES #2

Variety ad for the film when it was later renamed *The Primevals*.

giant ground sloth, which has a bridle attached to it like a horse! The men eventually come across a tribe of native peoples. There they find Hayward's daughter, Delandria, and the crew of the zeppelin, who have mysteriously gone mad since landing. Delandria tells Fulmer that her father went missing in the vicinity of a "stone city" some time ago.

As the men acclimate to life in the village, Easton learns to ride the ground sloth. While doing so, both confront and eventually drive away a giant lizard. Because of this act of heroism, the villagers agree to accompany the two outsiders to the Forbidden City in search of Hayward. The stone city is located inside of a mountain, and the heroes must pass through a waterfall to enter. Inside they find quite the plot twist in this prehistoric land: a crashed spaceship! There is also an ominous collection of human skulls.

Fulmer and Easton discover a breathtaking city, lit by cascades of light that shine through holes in the mountain. They find Hayward, who now has scaly skin and an odd way of speaking. He is able to tell the men that long ago a race of aliens crash landed here. They then took the DNA of the primitive peoples of the time to enhance themselves. This turned the peaceful aliens evil, as it turns out!

Fulmer and Eaton are eventually captured themselves to be altered as Hayward was. Naturally, they escape, so that they can rescue Delandria, who the aliens have also captured. The men manage to rescue her from the lizard-like aliens (who resemble what people in the UFO community would call Reptilians).

The zeppelin has been repaired by this point and makes a surprise entrance by dropping bombs on the aliens and their giant lizard protectors. The aliens are defeated, and Fulmer and Eaton both decide to stay in the lost land when the zeppelin prepares to return to the outside world.

Pre-production work began on the prospective film in the form of armatures and puppets for the aliens and the monsters. Notably, the designs for both were based on previous unmade films. The aliens at this point in development were

43

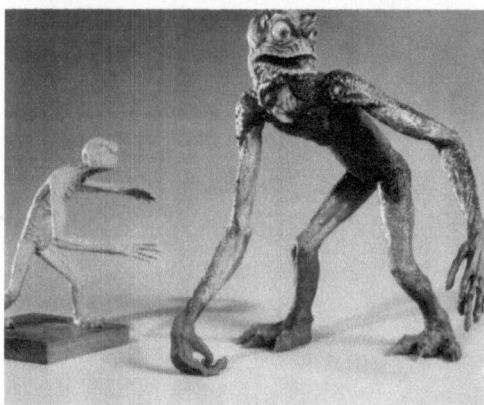

One of Allen's armatures of the Lizard Men.

made to resemble the aliens from *The Beetlemen*, an abandoned project of Pete Peterson (a stopmotion animator best known for helping on *Mighty Joe Young* and *The Black Scorpion*). The giant lizard was built over a leftover armature from Willi's O'Brien's scrapped Western monster movie *The Last of the Oso Si-Papu*.

What we would today call a Sizzler Reel (a specially shot trailer meant to look as though it's for a finished film) was shot in Southern California. This was done as an attempt to impress Hammer, who had yet to greenlight the project (or to impress other prospective investors should Hammer pass).

Hammer was interested, but knew they couldn't afford to produce it. In an effort to make the story less sci-fi, and also as a way of reducing the budget, Hammer suggested cutting the aliens altogether. They also suggested the new title of *Creatures the World Forgot* (similar to *The Land That Time Forgot*). They suggested that the aliens be a second tribe of men in "strange headgear" which would evolve into the Mud Men in the movie Hammer eventually did make called *Creatures the World Forgot* in 1971. It's rather bizarre in hindsight that the ambitious *Raiders of the Stone Ring* helped lead to the production of Hammer's least ambitious caveman film!

Allen in particular didn't want to abandon his original vision, and understandably so. Though some bartering and palavering took place up until as late as April of 1971 (when *Creatures* was seeing theatrical release), Hammer and Allen eventually gave up on *Zeppelin vs. Pterodactyls/Raiders of the Stone Ring*. Happily and remarkably, the project evolved into *The Primevals* and the live action footage was shot in 1994. The project is still in development today, and looks to be released within the next few years by Full Moon Entertainment.

Back to the development of *Creatures*, artwork by Tom Chantrell created three concept posters for the film before it was made. One showed a large, three eyed skull. To the side, a woman was being whipped by a man with an elongated skull. The tagline referred to the beings as "the Unknowns." It also proclaimed that they were a "super-race without guilt, compassion, or morals" and that they had an "invisible sixth sense."

It's my guess that this poster was based on the ZvP idea at the time when Carreras wanted to replace the aliens with "men in strange headgear." Chantrell's other poster depicted a topless woman front and center flanked by people in what looked to be tight fitting futuristic clothing. The third poster featured primitive men in strange headgear, or the "Mud Men," as they would be termed in the completed film.

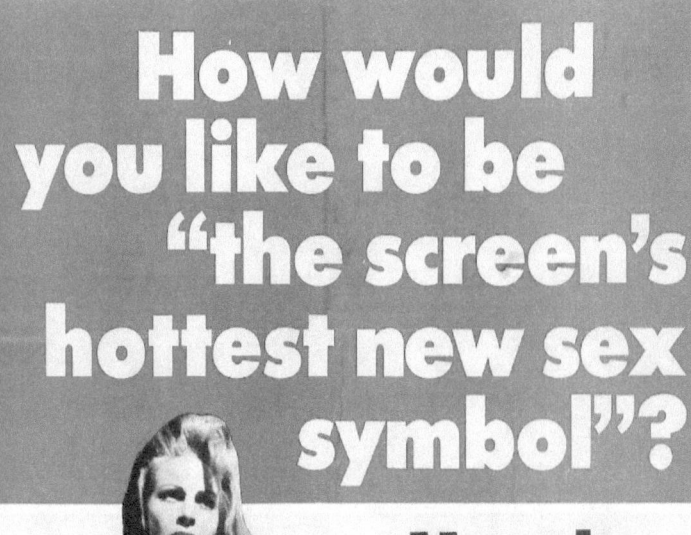

Above: Tom Chantrell's concept poster for the film. Top Right: Lobby Card depicting the Mud Men about to harm Toomak's brother. Right: Julie Ege poses with the terrible prehistoric bear suit. Previous pages: Hammer Ad Campaign to find the next Raquel Welch, and Tom Chantrell's concept poster. (with nudity censored by the editor)

Interestingly, Marcus Hearn's *Hammer Vault* reports that Anthony Hinds wrote a *Creatures the World Forgot* script, but unfortunately what it entailed is unknown. At the same time, *Horror of Frankenstein* writer Jeremy Burnham submitted a script under that title that reads suspiciously like Allen's *Raiders* idea. The lizardmen are replaced by batmen who are discovered living in the catacombs of a volcano. Carreras then rechristened that script *The Day the Earth Cracked Open*, which we'll return to later.

Ultimately, Carreras did away with all of the previous script's batmen, lizardmen, and monsters to write what more or less became a dinosaur-free remake of *One Million* B.C. In the place of dinosaurs, the film sports a very shoddy prehistoric bear, a python, and the Mud Men. The latter descended from the aliens in *Zeppelins vs. Pterodactyls*, who Carreras wanted to downsize into "men in strange headgear." And indeed, the Mud Men's headgear is strange. The trailer describes them as "primordial devils" and "gods of the forest" though they appear to simply be a violent tribe of men coated in mud and wearing huge head pieces.

To call the film's storytelling episodic would be a bit of an understatement. The first half of the film centers on the main character's parents.

The German poster succinctly titled this film *Sex 6 Million Years Ago*, while the Japanese poster showed a topless Marcia Fox.

The movie begins with a volcanic eruption, mostly courtesy of the '66 *B.C.* stock footage mixed with new shots of pyrotechnics blasting off behind the cast. The eruption decimates the home of this film's version of the Rock Tribe, though it seems to be officially designated as the Dark Tribe.

The Dark Tribe, led by Mak (Brian O'Shaughnessy), wanders across the unforgiving desert (and the locales are striking) until they come across a more peaceful tribe of fair-haired people. The two tribes intermarry, and a rather arcane, ritualized mating ceremony takes place in an effort to come across as shocking.

Eventually twin boys are born to Mak, while on the same day a mute girl is born to another woman. For some unexplained reason, the tribe wants to sacrifice or kill the girl, but lightning strikes a nearby tree. The tribe's female shaman decrees the girl is to live, and takes her as her apprentice.

The rest of the film then hinges upon the strange circumstances of the birth of the two boys and the girl. The fair haired boy is named Toomak, a variation on the spelling of Tumak (perhaps changed so as not to owe any royalties to original *One Million B.C.* producer Hal Roach?). Toomak's brother is dark haired and named Rool. His cruel treatment of the mute girl makes it clear he's the villain.

After spending some time with the three kids as pre-teens, we skip to the future where we finally meet the touted stars of the film, Tony Bonner as Toomak, Robert John as Rool, and Marcia Fox as the unnamed mute girl.

We are by now about half way into the movie when a series of events sets the true story into motion (finally). The mute girl is kidnapped by a rival tribe, and Mak's tribe goes to rescue her from their cave lair. In the process, Toomak finds the woman Nala.

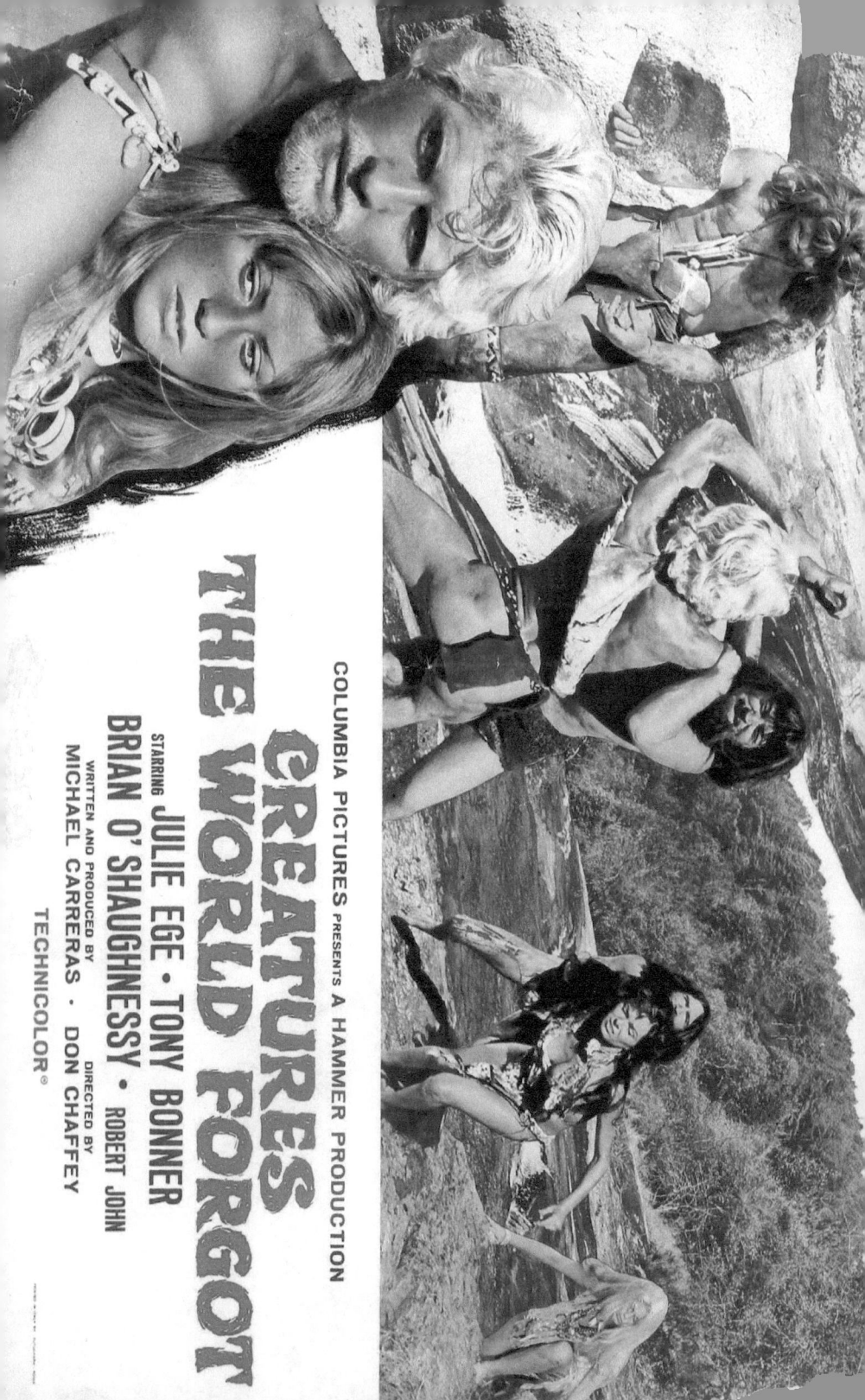

Previous two pages and top image: Lobby Card set for *CTWF*. Right: Publicity image of Julie Ege.

Nala, played by Julie Ege, was the central focus in the advertising campaign, so it's a bit strange that she doesn't show up until 56 minutes into the 95 minute film! Soon after Toomak takes Nala for a mate, Mak dies, meaning Toomak and Rool must fight it out to decide who the new leader is. Toomak wins, shaming his brother. The tribe splinters in two, with Toomak leading the larger portion off to greener pastures.

But, the brothers' paths cross again when Rool's group is attacked by the mysterious Mud Men while in the forest. Toomak's tribe comes to their rescue, but this does nothing to quell Rool's jealousy, as he uses the chaotic situation to abduct Nala.

Toomak chases Nala and Rool across a long stretch of river rock. (Interestingly enough, this scene was copied in the Bollywood caveman film *Aadi Yug* for its climax too.) Eventually Toomak catches up to Rool, who has tied Nala to a rock. While the brothers wrestle, Nala fends off a python.

Meanwhile, the mute girl stabs a tiny prehistoric voodoo doll of Rool, causing him to fall to his death! Overall, it's a strange little ending that requires the viewer to do some "fill in the blank"-type thinking to make sense of it all.

The film was shot in the Namib Desert rather than the Canary Islands again because Carreras had done location scouting there for an aborted Hammer TV series called *Safari*. *B.C.*'s Don Chaffey returned to direct as did composer Nascimbene, who composes a score more reminiscent of *B.C.* than *WDRTE*.

It would seem that *CTWF* was an experiment of sorts on Hammer's part to see if they even needed the dinosaurs, instead touting the film's leading beauty.

Despite being touted as a new star discovery in the trailers, Ege was not a newcomer to cinema and had appeared in numerous films in small parts, notably as one of Blofeld's beauties in *On Her Majesty's Secret Service*. She also submitted a photo of herself for Hammer's contest "The Sex Symbol of the 1970s" and generated a lot of publicity for 1970's *Every Home Should Have One* which caught Hammer's eye.

Before she knew it Ege was being worked over by the Hammer publicity machine as their newest star discovery with promises of becoming the next Raquel Welch. Ege didn't have the best of luck on *CTWF*, however. Though she got to wear a fur bikini, she didn't get the glamour treatment that Raquel Welch, Victoria Vetri, or even *Prehistoric Women's* Martine Beswick did. Ege was instead presented as a very dirty realistic cave woman with tangled hair. She's also not on camera much.

I almost feel like there's a lost version of *CTWF*, one actually starring Julie Ege. I was confounded when I first saw the film because Ege wasn't emphasized a great deal. Her character shows up at about an hour in, well over halfway, and the camera doesn't give her a lot of love compared to co-star Marcia Fox. In reading an interview with Ege in *Little Shoppe of Horrors* #15, I finally learned why.

As Ege tells it, she had recently given birth and was depressed to be separated from her newborn child, nor did she always feel very well. As a result she turned in early after shooting while the rest of the crew stayed up late partying. One of the cameramen took it the wrong way assuming that Ege was a snob and purposely kept her out of shot during filming whenever possible, somewhat explaining why she doesn't have a large presence in the film. In the interview with *Little Shoppe of Horrors* Ege said, "When the daily rushes were looked upon back in London the producers were furious and told them to focus on me." [pp.35]

However, Ege was still the lynch pin of the advertising, including the all-important poster, and did a sizeable amount of publicity for the film even appearing on the *Tonight Show* with Johnny Carson. *CTWF* was released in the UK with an X certificate (it has since been given a PG rating) where it had a respectable first week of business before it dropped off the radar. Critics had surprisingly nice things to say about it when it premiered in America later in September. Howard Thompson of the *New York Times* said, "At about mid-point, the colour photographer, or director—or whoever was grunting and groaning behind the camera, starts doing some interesting things with the exotic African terrain." Thompson went on to compliment Nascimbene's score and called the whole picture better than *B.C.*!

Though it might be an inauspicious end to Hammer's cavepeople pictures, if one can get over the fact that there's no dinosaurs (and excuse the awful cave bear!), *CTWF* is an interesting little film. And, if not for its more ambitious siblings, the film might be remembered as one of the better cavepeople pictures of its day.

ADVERTISING AIDS

Ad No. 201—420 Lines—2 Cols. x 15 Inches

Ad No. 301—330 Lines—3 Cols. x 7⅞ Inches

Ad No. 302—270 Lines—3 Cols. x 6⅔ Inches

Page 2

COLUMBIA PICTURES PRESENTS
A HAMMER PRODUCTION
CREATURES THE WORLD FORGOT

AN UNFORGETTABLE WORLD OF UNIMAGINABLE SAVAGERY

SEE the devil gods of the primeval jungle!
SEE the most titanic earthquake ever filmed!
SEE the terrifying ordeal of the virgins!
SEE the flaming torch against the naked blade!
SEE the sensational new star Julie Ege. She's a creature you'll never forget.

starring JULIE EGE / TONY BONNER / BRIAN O'SHAUGHNESSY / ROBERT JOHN
Written and Produced by MICHAEL CARRERAS / Directed by DON CHAFFEY / TECHNICOLOR®

Ad No. 401—480 Lines—4 Cols. x 8½ Inches

ACCESSORIES
- ONE SHEET
- THREE SHEET
- SIX SHEET
- INSERT CARD
- 22 x 28
- WINDOW CARD
- EIGHT 11 x 14's
- UTILITY MAT
- AD MATS
- HI-RISE STANDEE
- TRAILER
- 40 x 60, 24 x 60, 24 x 82, 30 x 40
- STILL SETS
(Color and B. W—Color, for lobby and store displays; B/W stills for newspaper planting)

From National Screen

Order From
Exploitation Dept.
Columbia Pictures
711 5th Ave., N. Y. 10022

RADIO SPOTS
TV SPOTS

UTILITY MAT NO. 1
- Ad No. 102
- Ad No. 103
- Ad No. 104
- Ad No. 204
- Ad No. 205

Running Time:
95 Minutes

Aspect Ratio:
1:85

Ad No. 101—75 Lines
1 Col. x 5⅜ Inches

Ad No. 102—14 Lines
1 Col. x 1 Inch

Ad No. 205—100 Lines—2 Cols. x 3⅝ Inches

Ad No. 204—80 Lines—2 Cols. x 2⅝ Inches

APPROVED

All advertising in this pressbook, as well as all other advertising and publicity materials referred to herein, has been approved under the standards for Advertising of the Code of Self-Regulation of the Motion Picture Association of America. All inquiries on this procedure may be addressed to:

Director of the Code for Advertising
Motion Picture Association of America
522 Fifth Avenue, N. Y., N. Y. 10036

THE LOST FILMS FANZINE PRESENTS MOVIE MILESTONES #2

WHEN THE EARTH CRACKED OPEN

Despite *CTWF's* lukewarm reception at the box office, Hammer still toyed with more prehistoric adventures from time to time. There were about three different concepts considered. One project was simply another mystery prehistoric adventure, of which we know not the title or the concept.

As late as 1974 Hammer was still thinking about their films set during prehistory. This one had a twist too. If you'll recall, in the early 1970s, Hammer amped up the occult content in their Dracula films, particularly the last two entries to team Lee and Cushing that were set in the 1970s. Hammer decided to go this route with an unmade caveman picture called *Stones of Evil*, which would have explored Stonehenge's pagan origins via cave people in the prehistoric past. (Even *Creatures the World Forgot* has a semi-arcane wedding ceremony of sorts in it).

The Encyclopedia of Hammer Film's appendix entry for the project states, "In 2600 B.C., travelling stonemason encounters evil Druid priest at Stonehenge. Based on 1974 novel by Bryan Cooper."

But, before the two projects I briefly just outlined were even thought up, Hammer had another grand prehistoric adventure in mind tentatively titled *When the Earth Cracked* open.

The story's genesis was similar to the bizarre developmental process of *CTWF*, which bounced back and

Tom Chantrell's poster featured a rather demonic looking creature, perhaps it was inspired by the aborted bat-men? (Nudity censored by editor)

forth between being set in the future and the prehistoric past. It began as a spec script (called *The Day the Earth Cracked Open* rather than *When*) by Don Houghton in the late 1960s. He first pitched it to Amicus, who may not have been interested because they were trying to adapt the Burroughs stories (these efforts began in the mid-1960s even if they didn't see fruition until 1974). Houghton's idea was a futuristic monster adventure.

There were other *Days the Earth Cracked Open* on Carreras's desk, and I'm not sure how they related to Houghton's. According to *The Hammer Vault*, one was written by Nadja Regin (Hammer's script reader). It opened during WWII and had a British soldier about to be executed by the Nazis. He is saved when the ground swallows him up and he disappears. He is found in the present day by tourists who have become lost in an underground labyrinth. The underground world is ruled by fearsome cannibals who believe the long lost soldier is a "fire god."

Then there was Jeremy Burnham's story about a race of batmen who live under a volcano, which Carreras gave the title of *The Day the Earth Cracked Open* (I'm not sure what Burnham called it himself).

Carreras passed these ideas over in favor of Houghton's in 1969. (If you'll remember, at that time Carreras was very excited by what he was seeing in terms of Danforth's animation on *WDRTE*. As such, he wanted to produce more adventure movies.) Conversely, *The Encyclopedia of Hammer Films* states that Houghton's screenplay was based upon Regin and Burnham's stories, and also lists Anthony Hinds as part of the creative milieu.

Whoever wrote it, Sir James Carreras wasn't crazy about it. A March 9, 1972 letter from Sir James to son Michael would seem to confirm that *Cracked Open* began as either a future-set or modern day adventure. The letter read,

"I don't think... it's very good... I really couldn't care less what happens to these with-it bods in the holiday camp, or the local village.

I think that the earthquake and the type of monsters and what they get up to, is quite good, and had all this happened to Raquel Welch and all her friends in a setting of a million years ago, then it could be quite good.

Is it possible to shift the plot to that time period? I know they'd have to fight the monsters in different ways, but I don't like the modern setting."

And indeed this is what Hammer did. *Harryhausen: The Lost Movies* has an entire entry on *When the Earth Cracked Open*. According to that book, Harryhausen was approached in 1971, which curiously predates Sir James's letter. In Harryhausen's *An Animated Life* book, he states that he was working with Houghton to develop the story in late 1970.

The prospective film was to begin with a special effects montage of man's development through the Ice Age until its end. At that point, in the days of early man and Neanderthals, the story would finally begin.

In the usual *B.C.* style, the story centered around two distinct tribes, the River People and the Fire Warriors. One day, while the River tribe's leader Rabbala goes out on a fishing trip with his men, the River Camp is raided by the Fire Warriors, led by the wicked Za'ama. They kill the elderly and the children, and kidnap all the women.

From here, it becomes a quest story, with Rabbala and his men on a journey to the lair of the Fire Warriors, simple enough. Their journey would take them through what Harryhausen called the Poison Swamp. Within the swamp they would encounter a giant toad and some sort of tentacled creature (apparently not an octopus, or Harryhausen likely would have identified it as such).

The River People make it through the swamp and pick up the trail of the Fire Warriors in a barren desert. There they would be attacked by another giant monster, of which Harryhausen had several different options for, including a giant sand crab, an ankylosaurus, a triceratops, a giant sloth, or a giant armored beetle.

THE LOST FILMS FANZINE PRESENTS MOVIE MILESTONES #2

Production sketches also show a giant lizard emerging from the ground to menace the men too, although I'm not sure exactly where this scene was to take place. This is a good spot to note that Harryhausen so loved Danforth's mother dinosaur from *WDRTE* that he planned to use a similar design on a giant lizard creature. The creature in
the artwork is quasi-similar to the mother dinosaur, so that must've been it. As for the creature emerging from the ground, I wonder if this was a nod to Harryhausen's cancelled *Deluge* remake, wherein he envisioned monsters emerging from the ground? Despite Harryhausen acting as though the picture was prehistoric, his pre-production drawings show men in modern clothing confronting the lizard monster. The image to the right shows a cobra-like serpent. Harryhausen had snakes on the brain at the time, and also tried to integrate giant snakes into 1973's *The Golden Voyage of Sinbad* to no avail.

Similar to a scene from *King Kong*, the giant whatever-it-was would chase them over a gorge and into a jungle. There they would be attacked by giant soldier ants (presumably inspired by *WDRTE's* aborted ant scene). An intense rain storm would wash the critters away.

For their next challenge, the group encounters a lake made up entirely of salt and sulfur. Within it lurks a serpentine creature and an animal that Houghton envisioned as a cross between an ape and a lizard (according to Harryhausen the beast would be played for laughs).

The story would end at the Fire Warrior's lair, near a volcano (naturally). Rabbala and his men push huge rocks into the volcanic crater causing an eruption so intense that it fulfills the movie's title when it splits the Earth open. During the chaos, the River Men would rescue the River Women, and

Above: Coulda been a Cavegirl. This being a film in the B.C. genre, *When the Earth Cracked Open* also needed a fine leading lady. In this case, Caroline Munro would have starred had the film actually gone before cameras. Though she never played one for Hammer, she did play a cavegirl/princess in Amicus's *At the Earth's Core* (1976). **Right: Tom Chantrell's futuristic concept poster edited for modesty.**

the volcano would consume the Fire Warriors. In the words of *Harryhausen: The Lost Movies* the finale was to have "walls of lava and volcanoes."

As with *CTWF*, Chantrell did three concept posters that we know of. All three had topless women. The first showed a woman in a fishbowl type helmet with a destroyed city behind her. The second had a cavewoman with a volcano behind her and a demonic monster in the background that certainly wasn't a dinosaur. The third curiously had a jellyfish like alien ensnaring a woman in its tentacles underwater.

Over the course of revisions, it was eventually decided to do only four stopmotion pieces. Perhaps to set it apart from *B.C.* the potential dinosaurs were excised. The four monster pieces would include a swamp monster (possibly a giant saurian of some kind, but possibly the tentacled creature), a giant stag beetle, the giant ants (possibly to use the armatures built for *WDRTE*), and a giant armadillo (presumably a glyptodont).

In later years, Harryhausen stated that perhaps the film was better unmade in his *Animated Life*. He wrote, "Reading [the treatment] today, the whole thing looks like One Million Years B.C. Part II, and perhaps its best that it was never realized." On the other hand, in *The Art of Ray Harryhausen* he lamented its abandonment: "Neither project came to fruition and I am not too sad about [the Kong remake], but [*When the Earth Cracked Open*] did

THE LOST FILMS FANZINE PRESENTS MOVIE MILESTONES #2

WDRTE has one other lost-film quasi-cousin in the form of Hammer's infamous *Nessie*, and it's not just because it was to star a dinosaur. As all lost film aficionados know, the film was to be a joint production with Hammer and Godzilla's home studio of Toho in Japan. But, before Toho came on board, Michael Carreras had ideas of re-teaming two of the creative powerhouses behind *WDRTE*. He envisioned Jim Danforth doing the special effects and Val Guest directing. This idea didn't last terribly long, as eventually other directors like Bryan Forbes were brought on and it was decided Toho could produce the effects faster than Danforth could. While *Nessie* would never make it to screens, Danforth did help with the production of 1977's *The Crater Lake Monster* about an elasmosaurus in a lake. Had *Nessie* actually been produced, it would have seen the famous Loch Ness Monster mutated by a radioactive steroid! It would then escape the loch and cause chaos across Earth's oceans until it meets a fiery, tragic end in Hong Kong harbor.

have some possibilities.... I did rough out some basic ideas as storyboards of giant ants, dinosaurs and a tentacled beast but that's as far as it went." [pp.76]

At the time, it was hoped Hammer could entice AIP to distribute. Carreras had asked Anthony Hinds for a revision, which he did with no regard for budget whatsoever.

In *An Animated Life*, Harryhausen reported that the last communication he had on the project was in July of 1971. Michael Carreras informed him that "the production of this subject has, for various reasons, had to be postponed until Spring of next year."

But that wasn't the end of the project. By 1973, the prehistoric aspect had been dropped again and the setting had shifted back to the present. Hinds' idea to make the title literal was that an offshore oil rig drills too deep into the earth. Water leaks to the magma beneath the earth's crust which causes a huge explosion, followed by earthquakes, tsunamis, and other disasters. It was at this point that Carreras finally kyboshed the project.

THE LOST FILMS FANZINE PRESENTS MOVIE MILESTONES #2

AFTER DINOSAURS RULED THE EARTH

Above and Right: Still and poster from *When Women Had Tails*. Next page: Poster for *WWHT*'s imitator and sequel.

Oddly, neither the 1966 *B.C.* nor *Prehistoric Women* ushered in a great deal of copycat films that pre-dated *WDRTE*. The only one of note was Ed Wood's softcore porn spoof *One Million AC/DC*. There was no real plot to speak of, and in between softcore sex scenes the cavemen fight a very fake looking T-rex (from that same year's *The Mighty Gorga*) that has trapped them all within their cave.

More notable were the post *WDRTE* releases, the first of which was *When Women Had Tails*, a title clearly modeled after *WDRTE* as opposed to *B.C.* Considering this sex comedy came out only a few days after *WDRTE* on October 15, 1970, one has to wonder if it was a coincidence or if the film was produced in anticipation of *WDRTE's* presumed success.

The story concerns a group of seven brothers (I assume a nod to *Seven Brides for Seven Brothers*) who stumble upon the first woman they've ever seen (they became separated from their mother when they were too young to remember her). This strange creature looks like them only prettier, but has a tail (yes, she really does have a tail, by the way). At first the men plan to eat

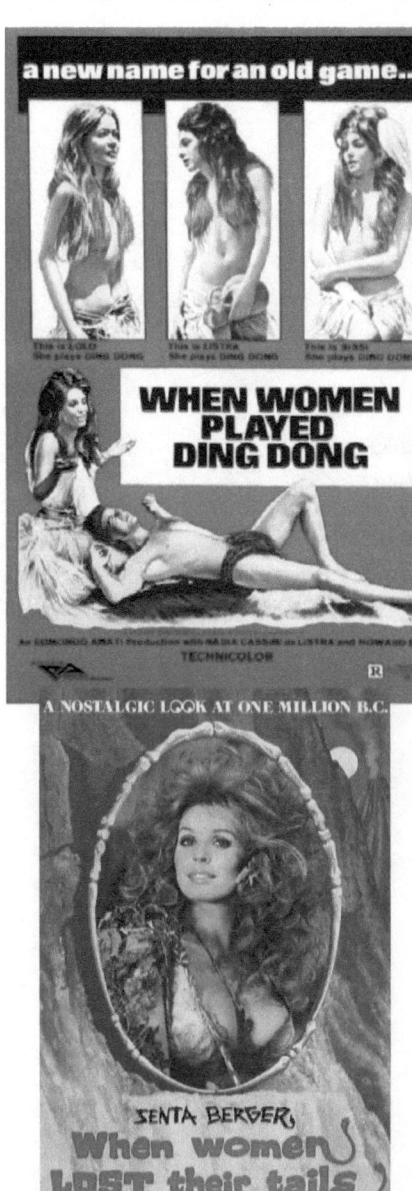

bargained for when they find Filli's all-female tribe of over 100 women, all of whom want to make lovers out of the five cavemen, who are about to be seriously over worked.

Though certainly dated, the film actually is funny at times. This is thanks in large part to the fact that the cavemen speak and have dialogue, unlike the *B.C.* films. One of the funnier gags had one of the brothers eating a frog, which lives on in his stomach. To get rid of the frog, he eats a mouse. Then to get rid of the mouse he has to eat an owl! It's classic Italian type comedy, so if you like the Beans Westerns (comical Spaghettis) of the time, then you might like this one. Also, the score was composed by no less than Spaghetti Western maestro Ennio Morricone!

If your interest is more in the prehistoric realm, there are no dinosaurs or real prehistoric beasts to speak of, though I might assume it was because there wasn't any money for them. Dinosaurs are mentioned a couple of times, and a cave bear only slightly worse than the one that appeared in *CTWF* pops up.

Austrian born Senta Berger is every bit as voluptuous as Raquel Welch was in *B.C.* and makes an excellent impression as Filli. Ulli, the male lead, is played by Giuliano Gemma. Gemma was comparable to Italian superstar Terrence Hill in that he started out as an action-western star before becoming more of a comedy player (Gemma even replaced Hill in *Even Angels Eat Beans* alongside Bud Spencer).

the woman, named Filli, but one of the brothers sets her free. She teaches him the joys of lovemaking for the first time. His brothers want in on the action, and so the lovers run away. The movie has a funny twist ending when the other brothers get more than they

WWHT apparently spawned its own imitators. The next year was produced the silly but still semi-explicitly titled *When Men Carried*

THE LOST FILMS FANZINE PRESENTS MOVIE MILESTONES #2

Above: Still from *Korg: 70,000 B.C.* Right: Misleading poster for *When Women Lost Their Tails.*

Clubs and Women Played Ding-Dong. It was based upon the Greek classic Lysistrata wherein women withheld sex from the men as a way of stopping a war. In this case, the women become fed up when the men of their tribe are more interested in making war with a rival tribe than they are in having sex, so the women go on a sex strike altogether. Like *WWHT*, there are no dinosaurs in this one either.

In 1972 came an official sequel in the form of *When Women Lost Their Tails.* The parameters of the sequel's continuity are unclear, as Berger returns as Filli, but not Gemma. In Ulli's absence, Filli is now the shared wife of the five brothers, (most of which are played by different actors but not all).

This one was heavier on the dinosaur references as the main characters actually live in a dinosaur skeleton (but still no live dinosaurs). The main plot involved prehistoric real-estate development and Filli finding a new mate. I don't know if the film was a hit or not, but either way, thus ended Italy's brief run of prehistoric sex comedies.

In 1974, the cavepeople came to television in the form of a live-action Saturday morning series called *Korg: 70,000 B.C.* It was narrated by Burgess Meredith and lasted only one season.

Later came Bollywood's 1978 *B.C.* inspired *Aadi Yug*, or *Earliest Age*. The film doesn't seem to be sure if it's a straightforward caveman movie or a comedy, but you can pick out scenes throughout the picture that were obviously inspired by all three of Hammer's prehistoric epics. *Aadi Yug* even pilfers stock-footage from *One Million B.C.* (by then nearly 40 years old)! It was the last instance of stock footage from that movie being used in a serious context that I know of. The movie also borrowed illegally from one of Toho's monster movies: 1965's *Frankenstein Conquers the World*. In that film, a caveman-like giant Frankenstein monster had battled a dinosaur named Baragon, which is passed off as a normal-sized caveman vs. dinosaur fight in *Aadi Yug*. [see *Lost Films Fanzine #2* for a full rundown]

Right: Foreign release poster for *Caveman* depicting Ringo riding the T-Rex, something that he does not do in the film (he rides the horned lizard pictured directly above).

Though both the *Women Had Tails* films had been quasi-spoofs of Hammer's caveman movies, the big spoof didn't come until 1981 in the form of *Caveman*. The movie is notorious today for the fact that it's not terribly funny—at least not funny enough to carry a full-length feature. It's mostly remembered for the fact that it starred Ringo Starr and featured some wonderful and intentionally comical stopmotion work from the great Jim Danforth.

Caveman was written and directed by *Jaws* writer Carl Gottlieb. It began gestating in 1979 as *Caveman*, before changing to *Stone Age*, then reverting back to *Caveman*. The film has two major dinosaurs, one pterodactyl, and a walrus man. Of the two major dinosaurs, one was supposed to be a triceratops. The only problem was Gottlieb only referred to it as a "horned lizard" in his script, and so that's exactly what Danforth designed.

The film's tyrannosaurs rex is essentially designed as a decrepit, elderly saurian with a notable paunch and is hilarious. There's also a howling dinosaur that emulates either a coyote or a crow depending on the time of day that makes for a good gag too. (Interestingly, Danforth says the armature for the "howling lizard" was created by modifying an "unused Ceratosaurus" armature from *WDRTE*!)

There were also a few deleted dinos in the forms of a brachiosaurus and a triceratops, which were sculpted before they were written out of the film.

The pterodactyl scene is rather interesting. In it, the cavemen steal a giant egg from the nest before being attacked by the parent. When the egg drops from a high cliff, the ground below is so hot that it fries the gigantic egg! I find the scene interesting because it was similar to the aborted pterodactyl egg hunt from *WDRTE* (sans humor, of course). Though I wondered if the scene was Danforth's suggestion (recalling *WDRTE*), I don't think it was, for he says nothing about this scene being taken from WDRTE in his memoirs, *Dinosaurs, Dragons, & Drama*.

The film was a flop when finally released, and Siskel and Ebert claimed that there was "no popular original material for it to satirize. There has never been a really successful movie set in prehistoric times." This is doubly ironic, because not only were both versions of *B.C.* smash hits in their day, but 1981 also saw the release of the critically acclaimed caveman movie *Quest for Fire* (it came out months after *Caveman* to be clear). In hindsight, *Caveman* might have fared better if it was written and shot after *Quest for Fire's* release, so it could've spoofed something more popular from the era (the '66 *B.C.* was by then 15 years old).

As it turned out, *Caveman* would be the last big studio movie in the vein of cavepeople cohabitate with dinosaurs. Save for *Dinosaur Valley Girls*, Don Glut's beloved 1996 independent feature, future caveman films would stick closer to realism, having cavemen interact with Ice Age megafauna like mammoths (as in *Quest for Fire*). So far, the last modern attempt at such a film was Roland Emmerich's *10,000 B.C.* (2008), which, though not a giant hit, was still a moderate success at the box office.

Oddly enough, *Caveman* didn't kill spoofs of the genre, and in 1983 was produced *Grunt*, a comedy about cavemen worshipping a giant egg struck by lightning!

BIBLIOGRAPHY/SUGGESTED READING

This issue would not have been possible if not for the following tomes, some of which are currently out of print, like Jim Danforth's *Dinosaurs, Dragons, & Drama*. Happily, still in print are Mark F. Berry's classic *Dinosaur Filmography*, J.G Ballard's biography *Miracles of Life*, and the relatively new (and fantastic) *Harryhausen: The Lost Movies* by John Walsh. The single biggest source of information in this issue came from the prestigious *Little Shoppe of Horrors*, which devoted a whole issue (#41) to celebrating *When Dinosaurs Ruled the Earth*. If you'd like to read the most in-depth article on the making of *WDRTE* pick it up!!!

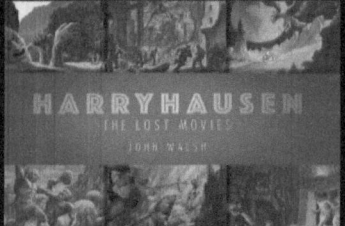  

ENJOYED REMINISCING ABOUT WHEN DINOSAURS RULED THE EARTH & CREATURES THE WORLD FORGOT?

BUY THE OFFICIAL RELEASES
WDRTE available on Blu-Ray from Warner Archive and *CTWF* available from Mill Creek on DVD

THE BICEP BOOKS CATALOGUE

The following titles are available for purchase on Amazon.com, and are available to bookstores at a wholesale discount via Ingram Content Group (ISBNs of available editions listed for this purpose)

THE BIG BOOK OF JAPANESE GIANT MONSTER MOVIES SERIES

The third edition of the book that started it all! Reviews over 100 tokusatsu films between 1954 and 1988. All the Godzilla, Gamera, and Daimajin movies made during the Showa era are covered plus lesser known fare like *Invisible Man vs. The Human Fly* (1957) and *Conflagration* (1975). Softcover (380 pp/5.83" X 8.27") Suggested Retail: $19.99 ISBN: 978-1-7341546-4-1

This third edition reviews over 75 tokusatsu films between 1989 and 2019. All the Godzilla, Gamera, and Ultraman movies made during the Heisei era are covered plus independent films like *Reigo, King of the Sea Monsters* and *Attack of the Giant Teacher*! Softcover (260 pp/5.83" X 8.27") Suggested Retail: $19.99 ISBN: 978-1-7347816-4-9

Covering unproduced scripts like *Bride of Godzilla* (1955), partially shot movies like *Giant Horde Beast Nezura* (1963), and banned films like *Prophecies of Nostradamus* (1974), this second edition of the Rondo Award nominated book covers hundreds of lost productions. 470 pp. Softcover/Hardcover (7" X 10") Suggested Retail: $24.99(sc)/$39.95(hc) ISBN: 978-1-7341546-0-3 (hc)

HUMOR

This sequel to *The Lost Films* covers the non-giant monster unmade movie scripts from Japan such as *Frankenstein vs. the Human Vapor* (1963), *After Japan Sinks* (1974-76), plus lost movies like *Fearful Attack of the Flying Saucers* (1956) and *Venus Flytrap* (1968). Hardcover (200 pp/5.83" X 8.27")/Softcover (216 pp/5.5" X 8.5") Suggested Retail: $9.99 (sc)/$24.99(hc) ISBN: 978-1-7341546-3-4 (hc)

This companion book to *The Lost Films* charts the development of all the prominent Japanese monster movies including discarded screenplays, story ideas, and deleted scenes. Also includes bios for writers like Shinichi Sekizawa, Niisan Takahashi and many others. Comprehensive script listing and appendices as well. Hardcover/Softcover (370 pp./6" X 9") Suggested Retail: $16.95(sc)/$34.99(hc) ISBN: 978-1-7341546-5-8 (hc)

Throughout the 1960s and 1970s the Italian film industry cranked out over 600 "Spaghetti Westerns" and for every *Fistful of Dollars* were a dozen pale imitations, some of them hilarious. Many of these lesser known Spaghettis are available in bargain bin DVD packs and stream for free online. If ever you've wondered which are worth your time and which aren't, this is the book for you. Softcover (160pp./5.06" X 7.8") Suggested Retail: $9.99

THE BICEP BOOKS CATALOGUE

MOVIES UNMADE SERIES

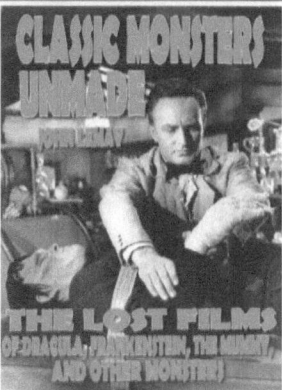

Kong Unmade explores unproduced scripts like *King Kong vs. Frankenstein* (1958), unfinished films like *The Lost Island* (1934), and lost movies like *King Kong Appears in Edo* (1938). As a bonus, all the Kong rip-offs like *Konga* (1961) and *Queen Kong* (1976) are reviewed. Hardcover (350 pp/5.83" X 8.27")/Softcover (376 pp/5.5" X 8.5") Suggested Retail: $24.99(hc)/$19.99 (sc) ISBN: 978-1-7341546-2-7(hc)

Jaws Unmade explores unproduced scripts like *Jaws 3, People 0* (1979), abandoned ideas like a Quint prequel, and even aborted sequels to Jaws inspired movies like *Orca Part II*. As a bonus, all the Jaws rip-offs like *Grizzly* (1976) and *Tentacles* (1977) are reviewed. Hardcover (316 pp/5.83" X 8.27")/Softcover (340 pp/5.5" X 8.5") Suggested Retail: $29.99(hc)/$17.95 (sc) ISBN: 978-1-7344730-1-8(hc)

Coming in 2021, *Classic Monsters Unmade* will cover lost and unmade films starring Dracula, Frankenstein, the Mummy and more monsters from Universal, Hammer, and beyond. Covers everything from *The Wolf Man vs. Dracula* to *Frankenstein vs. Godzilla*. Alternate versions of completed movies like *Frankenstein Meets the Wolfman* and *Horror of Dracula* will also be covered.

NOSTALGIA

Written at an intermediate reading level for the kid in all of us, these picture books will take you back to your youth. In the spirit of the old Ian Thorne books are covered *Giant Apes of the Movies*, *Dinosauruses of the Movies* and *Monster Insects of the Movies*.

Hardcover/Softcover (44 pp/7.5" X 9.25") Suggested Retail: $17.95(hc)/$9.99(sc) ISBN: 978-1-7341546-9-6 (hc) 978-1-7344730-5-6 (sc)

Hardcover/Softcover (44 pp/7.5" X 9.25") Suggested Retail: $17.95(hc)/$9.99(sc) ISBN: 978-1-7344730-6-3 (hc) 978-1-7344730-7-0 (sc)

Hardcover/Softcover (44 pp/7.5" X 9.25") Suggested Retail: $17.95(hc)/$9.99(sc) ISBN: 978-1-7347816-3-2 (hc) 978-1-7347816-2-5(sc)

THE BICEP BOOKS CATALOGUE

CRYPTOZOOLOGY/COWBOYS & SAURIANS

Cowboys & Saurians: Prehistoric Beasts as Seen by the Pioneers explores dinosaur sightings from the pioneer period via real newspaper reports from the time. Well-known cases like the Tombstone Thunderbird are covered along with more obscure cases like the Crosswicks Monster and more. Softcover (357 pp/5.06" X 7.8") Suggested Retail: $19.95 ISBN: 978-1-7341546-1-0

Cowboys & Saurians: Ice Age zeroes in on snowbound saurians like the Ceratosaurus of the Arctic Circle and a Tyrannosaurus of the Tundra, as well as sightings of Ice Age megafauna like mammoths, glyptodonts, Sarkastodons and Saber-toothed tigers. Tales of a land that time forgot in the Arctic are also covered. Softcover (264 pp/5.06" X 7.8") Suggested Retail: $14.99 ISBN: 978-1-7341546-7-2

Southerners & Saurians takes the series formula of exploring newspaper accounts of monsters in the pioneer period with an eye to the Old South. In addition to dinosaurs are covered Lizardmen, Frogmen, giant leeches and mosquitoes, and the Dingocroc, which might be an alien rather than a prehistoric survivor. Softcover (202 pp/5.06" X 7.8") Suggested Retail: $13.99 ISBN: 978-1-7344730-4-9

UFOLOGY/THE REAL COWBOYS & ALIENS IN CONJUNCTION WITH ROSWELL BOOKS

The Real Cowboys and Aliens: Early American UFOs explores UFO sightings in the USA between the years 1899-1864. Stories of encounters sometimes involved famous figures in U.S. history such as Lewis and Clark, and Thomas Jefferson. Hardcover (242pp/6" X 9") Softcover (262 pp/5.06" X 7.8") Suggested Retail: $24.99 (hc)/$15.95(sc) ISBN: 978-1-7341546-8-9 (hc)/978-1-7344730-8-7 (sc)

The second entry in the series, Old West UFOs, covers reports spanning the years 1865-1895. Includes tales of Men in Black, Reptilians, Spring-Heeled Jack, Sasquatch from space, and other alien beings, in addition to the UFOs and airships. Hardcover (276 pp/6" X 9") Softcover (308 pp/5.06" X 7.8") Suggested Retail: $29.95 (hc)/$17.95 (sc) ISBN: 978-1-7344730-0-1 (hc)/ 978-1-7344730-2-5 (sc)

The third entry in the series, The Coming of the Airships, encompasses a short time frame with an incredibly high concentration of airship sightings between 1896-1899. The famous Aurora, Texas, UFO crash of 1897 is covered in depth along with many others. Hardcover (196 pp/6" X 9") Softcover (222 pp/5.06" X 7.8") Suggested Retail: $24.99 (hc)/$15.95 (sc) ISBN: 978-1-7347816-1-8 (hc)/ 978-1-7347816-0-1(sc)

BACK ISSUES

THE LOST FILMS FANZINE

ISSUE #1 SPRING 2020 The lost Italian cut of *Legend of Dinosaurs and Monster Birds* called *Terremoto 10 Grado*, plus *Bride of Dr. Phibes* script, *Good Luck! Godzilla*, the King Kong remake that became a car commercial, Bollywood's lost *Jaws* rip-off, Top Ten Best Fan Made Godzilla trailers plus an interview with Scott David Lister. 60 pages. Three variant covers/editions (premium color/basic color/b&w)

ISSUE #2 SUMMER 2020 How 1935's *The Capture of Tarzan* became 1936's *Tarzan Escapes*, the Orca sequels that weren't, Baragon in Bollywood's *One Million B.C.*, unmade *Kolchak: The Night Stalker* movies, *The Norliss Tapes*, *Superman V: The New Movie*, why there were no *Curse of the Pink Panther* sequels, *Moonlight Mask: The Movie*. 64 pages. Two covers/editions (basic color/b&w)

ISSUE #3 FALL 2020 Blob sequels both forgotten and unproduced, *Horror of Dracula* uncut, *Son of Frankenstein* in color, myths of the lost *King Kong* Spider-Pit sequence debunked, the *Carnosaur* novel vs. the movies, *Terror in the Streets/Vampire Doll* 50th anniversary, *Bride of Godzilla* 55th Unniversary, Lee Powers sketchbook. 100 pages. Two covers/editions (basic color/b&w)

MOVIE MILESTONES

ISSUE #1 AUGUST 2020 Debut issue of *Movie Milestones*, celebrating 80 years of *One Million B.C.* (1940), and an early 55th Anniversary for *One Million Years B.C.* (1966). Abandoned ideas, casting changes, and deleted scenes from both films are highlighted during the developmental process, plus unmade projects related to both films are covered including *Before Adam*, *Mistress of the Seas*, a *Deluge* remake, and an axed *B.C.* TV series. Lesser known cavepeople pictures like Mexico's *The Beautiful Dreamer* (1952) and *Eegah* (1962) are covered as well. Plus, a mini-B.C. stock-footage filmography! Three collectible covers/editions (premium color/basic color/b&w)

NEXT ISSUE:

GORGO! KONGA! REPTILICUS! THE MONSTERS OF 1961 TURN 60!!!!

www.ingramcontent.com/pod-product-compliance
Lightning Source LLC
Chambersburg PA
CBHW020547080526
44583CB00013B/1043